1,000 Ways in 1,000 Days to Win from Within!™

Inspirational Insights for Your Life's Journey

Darryl S. Doane
Rose D. Sloat

Illustrations by Roger E. Hollis

Foreword by Krish Dhanam, Global Ambassador for the Zig Ziglar Group of Companies

Copyright © 2017 by Darryl S. Doane and Rose D. Sloat

All rights reserved. No part of this publication may be reproduced or transmitted in any form or by any means, electronic or mechanical, including photocopying, recording, or by information storage and retrieval system, without written permission from the publisher.

Published by: HRD Press, Inc.
 22 Amherst Road
 Amherst, MA 01002
 (413) 253-3488
 (800) 822-2801 (U.S. and Canada)
 (413) 253-3490 (fax)
 www.hrdpress.com

ISBN 978-1-61014-410-0

Production services by Jean Miller
Cover design by Eileen Klockars

Illustrations by Roger E. Hollis

Foreword by Krish Dhanam, Global Ambassador for the Zig Ziglar Group of Companies

Testimonials

Praise for *Win from Within* by Rose Sloat and Darryl Doane

"If we would only follow one of these beautiful thoughts, the world would be a better place. Great job!"

        Nancy Friedman, President,
        Telephone Doctor Customer Service
        Author, speaker, customer service and engagement expert
        www.nancyfriedman.com

"Rose and Darryl have done a magnificent job. They share with us 1,000 ways to recognize the beautiful truth—that all winning originates and must take place on the inside before it is expressed on the outside."

        Sandra Gallagher, President/CEO and Co-Founder
        Proctor Gallagher Institute

"Rose Sloat and Darryl Doane are very educated and experienced professionals who have mastered the art of improving one's self with others. I have had the privilege of getting to know both of them and see first-hand how to improve people's customer service skills as well as leadership and management levels. They also educate on sales training, time management, and even personal listening. Rose and Darryl complement each other in every way! Darryl has expressed that he wants to find the 'genius in everyone.' They leave an extraordinary, positive, and motivational 'wake' throughout the lives of the people they touch. Everyone who has heard them speak or read their magazines are better in the areas they specialize in. If training or development is a need, The Learning Service, Ltd. Is a must! Rose and Darryl are great people, making us beter by learning to Win from Within!"

        Amanda Smith, Account Executive

"Making the most of life's journey has been the bedrock of the years of work of Darryl and Rose. This collection of quotes and essays offer bitesize bits of insight and wisdom to provide inspiration and guidance along the way."

        David S. Doane, Ph.D.

"From his innermost being will flow rivers of living water."

        Bible translation of John 7:38
        New American Standard Version (1995)

Other books by authors Rose D. Sloat and Darryl S. Doane

HRD Press, Publisher:

Life's Journey—Find Your Place to Stand and Build the Right Future

Life's Journey—Find Your Place to Stand and Build the Right Future, Personal Journal

The Constant Customer—Keep them coming back again and again and again

Excuses, Excuses, Excuses—For Not Delivering Excellent Customer Service and What Should Happen

50 Activities for Achieving Excellent Customer Service

Stories They Will Remember

The New Sales Game, Facilitator's Guide

The New Sales Game, Participant Manual

AMACOM
American Management Association, AMA, Publisher

The Customer Service Activity Book: 50 Activities for Inspiring Exceptional Service

Self-Published

The Tiger & The Ringmaster—Taming High Tech with High Touch (available at https://www.createspace.com and at http://www.amazon.com

Former Publishers/Founders/Editors/ Primary Content Providers

Life's Journey—Professional and Personal Wholeness Magazine, www.lifesjourneymag.com

Dedication

To those who are passionately dedicated
to realizing and achieving
their purpose in life.

Contents

Foreword	xiii
Introduction	1
Illustration: Excellence	3
Insights #1 – #20	4
Illustration: Understand	9
Insights #21 – #40	10
Illustration: Embrace	15
Insights #41 – #60	16
Illustration: Courageous	21
Insights #61 – #80	22
Illustration: Reflection	27
Insights #81 – #100	28
Illustration: Satisfaction	33
Awareness Promotes Effectiveness: There are Always Alternatives to Consider	34
Insights #101 – #120	36
Illustration: Transcend	41
Insights #121 – #140	42
Illustration: Performance	47
Insights #141 – #160	48
Illustration: Direction	53
Insights #161 – #180	54
Illustration: Humanity	59
Insights #181 – #200	60
Illustration: Forward	65
Awareness Promotes Effectiveness Dreams and Goals All Begin from Within!	66
Insights #201 – #220	67

Illustration: Win	72
Insights #221 – #240	73
Illustration: Perception	78
Insights #241 – #260	79
Illustration: Serve	84
Insights #261 – #280	85
Illustration: Fulfill	90
Insights #281 – #300	91
Illustration: Heartfelt	96
Awareness Promotes Effectiveness: Be a Gentle Soul	97
Insights #301 – #320	98
Illustration: Respect	103
Insights #321 – #340	104
Illustration: Explore	109
Insights #341 – #360	110
Illustration: Cheerful	115
Insights #361 – #380	116
Illustration: Master	121
Insights #381 – #400	122
Illustration: Special	127
Awareness Promotes Effectiveness: Choose Amazing and Stay Your Course!	128
Insights #401 – #420	129
Illustration: Wow	134
Insights #421 – #440	135
Illustration: Harmony	140
Insights #441 – #460	141
Illustration: Obsession	146
Insights #461 – #480	147

Illustration: Success	152
Insights #481 – #500	153
Illustration: Catapult	158
Awareness Promotes Effectiveness: Give More than You Take! Embrace the Right People!	159
Insights #501 – #520	161
Illustration: Devious	166
Insights #521 – #540	167
Illustration: Delve	172
Insights #541 – #560	173
Illustration: Gentleness	178
Insights #561 – #580	179
Illustration: Rejoice	184
Insights #581 – #600	185
Illustration: Confidence	190
Awareness Promotes Effectiveness: Fortress or Prison?	191
Insights #601 – #620	192
Illustration: Expectations	197
Insights #621 – #640	198
Illustration: Gifts	203
Insights #641 – #660	204
Illustration: Reaffirm	209
Insights #661 – #680	210
Illustration: Catalyst	215
Insights #681 – #700	216
Illustration: Ignite	221
Awareness Promotes Effectiveness: It Will Never Be the Same Again!	222
Insights #701 – #720	223

Illustration: Refocus	228
Insights #721 – #740	229
Illustration: Permit	234
Insights #741 – #760	235
Illustration: Advantage	240
Insights #761 – #780	241
Illustration: Climb	246
Insights #781 – #800	247
Illustration: Supposed	252
Awareness Promotes Effectiveness: 　　Life is a Puzzle!	253
Insights #801 – #820	255
Illustration: Challenge	260
Insights #821 – #840	261
Illustration: Music	266
Insights #841 – #860	267
Illustration: Foundation	272
Insights #861 – #880	273
Illustration: Vulnerable	278
Insights #881 – #900	279
Illustration: Force	284
Awareness Promotes Effectiveness: 　　Your Perception of Self!	285
Insights #901 – #920	286
Illustration: Conducive	291
Insights #921 – #940	292
Illustration: Willpower	297
Insights #941 – #960	298
Illustration: Devoted	303
Insights #961 – #980	304

Illustration: Mediocrity	309
Insights #981 – #1,000	310
Illustration: Act	315
Awareness Promotes Effectiveness: Abundance Come to Me!	316
About the Authors	317
About the Illustrator	318

Foreword

by Krish Dhanam

I am honored and privileged to have been asked to write some words to lend my voice to a superb narrative. Having been part of a journey that began as a migrant and one that culminated at the highest points of societal and cultural interaction, I am grateful for the request, but nervous about the ability to do it justice. From Chinese proverbs to existential expression, and from artistic renderings to dramatic revelations, we as a culture have always found ways to describe our journey. History is filled with examples of the process, and mystery has left some of the steps to imagination. Throughout time, man has always wanted to do more than he was capable of, have more than he currently did, and be more for the sake of a legacy. As an author and a speaker, I am often asked the question as to whether there is a specific formula for success. My answer shocks some and confuses most because it actually is very simple. The outward achievement that is our ambition begins within. Overtly simplistic some might say, but actually very practical. My mentor and hero, the late great Zig Ziglar, reminded me time and again that you must first imagine the destination for the journey to have wonder.

1,000 Ways in 1,000 Days to Win From Within! gives you snippets of imagination to add to your arsenal of dreams and thus provides the pieces of the puzzle that make the whole vision possible. Thank you Darryl and Rose for such an innovative and practical guide. You remind us that there are many components to success, and it is the need of the hour to personally find the prices that make the puzzle personal as well. It is not a crime to want to achieve and not against the grain of humanity to want to excel. Fred Smith Sr. often said that humility is not thinking less of yourself, it is thinking less often of yourself. The book you are holding gives you the unique ability to find a thousand ways and actually gives you permission in a short-term world to make a life-long impact.

I recommend you internalize the ways, personalize the methods, and vocalize the application on a daily basis. As you convince yourself from within that the journey of a thousand miles begins with a single step, you will look within at what is, add from the process what is needed, and be able to see clearly as to what could be. I had a picture of Lady Liberty on a wall in a small room in South Eastern India. It was the destination. It took two decades to finally see it in the harbor in New York. There are a 1,000 ways. There are a 1,000 days. The common denominator in the journey is you. Now read how to Win from Within.

Krish Dhanam, Global Corporate Adjunct Ravi Zacharias Ministries and
 Managing Partner, Skylife Success   krish@skylifesuccess.com
Author of *The American Dream from an Indian Heart* and *Hard Headed and
 Soft Hearted*

Introduction

A fire must be constantly fed or it will eventually burn out. The flame that once burned brightly is slowly reduced to dying embers and then nothing. So to, you need to consistently feed and fuel your own internal fire.

This book is intended to assist you each day with your focus of attention. The book will remind you that there is a directional beacon and a map for you to follow your charted course. Reach into your inner being each day to find the strength, encouragement, conviction, and guidance to live your purpose, vision, and goals that move you forward in your life's journey. Feed that inner spirit with positive, uplifting messages to catapult you in the direction of your destiny.

When you feed your inner spirit with these insightful, caring, daily messages, you are throwing logs on the fire of that spirit to promote the burn! What is inside (the glow) will radiate outward to you and to others.

A thousand ways in a thousand days—to Win from Within! We have written 1,000 messages to keep you focused, committed, and on track with your purpose and right future. They, along with supportive inspirational insights and illustrations, are contained in our newest work.

Do you have "real eyes," to "realize" where the "real" lies? Not just going through the motions in your everyday existence, but staying focused and on track. For you can have 20/20 eyesight with no "vision." This work will provide a continuous drive to "deal with the real" and Journey on! Achieve that ah-ha "critical max" moment where all the elements of your wholeness come together each day as you embrace your destiny and right future.

Each written inspiration is a personal commitment and pledge to carry on and strengthen your focus of attention to enhance the quality and purpose of your life.

We have also included supportive and complementary drawings to cause you to think and reflect. They say a picture is worth a thousand words. Each one is open to your perception of where you are and where you want to be.

So please use these fire starters to Win from Within. You will find 1000 inspirational insights here to ignite and renew your enthusiasm each day to come and to keep you on target for success. Be amazing!

Journey on!

Darryl S. Doane and Rose D. Sloat
October 14, 2016

1,000 Ways in 1,000 Days to Win from Within!

Excellence

Dreams don't work
unless you do!

RE Hollis

Insight #1

Do not seek perfection but strive for "Excellence." We are *human* beings, not *perfect* beings.

Journey on!

Insight #2

When you are flustered or fall down and at times even fail, do it in a forward movement in the direction of your future.

Journey on!

Insight #3

Focus on your real self. Be true, genuine, honest, and straightforward with yourself. Only from this reality can one chart a true course.

Journey on!

Insight #4

Maintain a spirit of vigilance. Watch everything as you move along your life's path. You are a traveler and each day becomes the single most significant learning experience of your entire life—so far!

Journey on!

Excellence

Insight #5

Do not let your fears halt you in your tracks. Remember that FEAR often stands for:

> **F** – False
> **E** – Expectations
> **A** – Appearing
> **R** – Real

Journey on!

Insight #6

When you are called to your destiny, will you answer? It's your choice! Only you can give yourself permission to take the necessary actions to create your own future.

Journey on!

Insight #7

Listen and observe well. There are many invitations given to assist us in our travels, yet so often we do not hear and we do not see. As a result, we often deviate from the "right path."

Journey on!

Insight #8

Remember that to you, your life can be an open book if only you can read and understand what you have written.

Journey on!

Reality

Insight #9

Often, things along our travels do not make sense. Remember, a small item can make a huge difference in your life. Do not walk by greatness and never realize it.

Journey on!

Insight #10

Your mind will not always be clear when you think back on all the ground you have already covered; all the pages you have already written in the book of your life. However, every now and then you will recall a memory with striking clarity. Embrace it! Cherish it!

Journey on!

Insight #11

Who do you go to when you are tormented or when you have a serious concern? Those friends, coaches, guides, teachers, and mentors are incredibly important to identify and utilize as you make decisions that will set your course.

Journey on!

Insight #12

Move forward humbly and with gratitude for each discovery of self along your way.

Journey on!

Create

Insight #13

Be your own "advocate." If you don't take care of "you," nobody else will take care of "you." If you don't look out for "you," no one else will look out for "you." Before you can focus your attention on others or anything else for that matter, you must begin with "YOU."

Journey on!

Insight #14

You only have one journey to travel. Don't miss it! Celebrate how precious your Life's Journey is and realize what you have before you!

Journey on!

Insight #15

The opposite of love is not hate, but indifference or apathy. It's not caring and not putting yourself where you need to be when you need to be there. Only you can do it.

Journey on!

Insight #16

Take your journey! Others will attempt to take you on their journey. Remember, you don't have to go! It is your choice, your decision, your life!

Journey on!

Cherish

Insight #17

A wise person does not just wish and hope to find a life worth living. You make it that way!

Journey on!

Insight #18

Life's Journey is like walking through the freshly fallen snow. Every step shows and makes a difference as to where you have been and where you are going.

Journey on!

Insight #19

You have dignity, worth, and you are a quality human being. There's nobody like you in the world. Use that uniqueness and make your mark.

Journey on!

Insight #20

You each have a wondrous statement to make with your life. Some of you will pass on and never make that statement. What an incredible loss. Make your statement!

Journey on!

Understand

Understand

Life's Journey. It's not a spectator sport.
You can't sit on the bench and watch.

RE Hollis

Insight #21

One does not have to be ill in order to get better or to improve. What are you waiting for?

Journey on!

Insight #22

You can't just dream it, think about it, or say it. You have to believe it, embrace it, and give yourself permission to take action. Do it!

Journey on!

Insight #23

Where is it? How do I get there? I must find it. It is my destiny. It is my future.

Journey on!

Insight #24

You have genius within you. Why not have a genius for living your life.

Journey on!

Gratitude

Insight #25

All your life, don't you dare settle for mediocrity! Move forward, take charge, and be a person of action!
Journey on!

Insight #26

Lose, fail, surrender, but don't even consider those as possibilities. They should not be part of your makeup. Success, victory, and accomplishment are your destiny!
Journey on!

Insight #27

Don't be afraid to enter the storm because your course goes through it and beyond to your future. Sail your ship to that particular harbor that is your destiny.
Journey on!

Insight #28

Your heart and your passion at times will drive you beyond your reason. They can see beyond the known to the unknown. Reason at times cannot fathom this.
Journey on!

Choice

Insight #29

It is a secret of the universe to reach for the stars that will guide you on your journey. Realize that there is no cause that is more noble than to give your all to your life's journey.
Journey on!

Insight #30

You have many more pages left to write in the book of your life. Celebrate each page as it lights each step you take in the direction of your destiny.
Journey on!

Insight #31

When someone puts you down, uses verbal abuse, and doesn't support you, stay the course and leave the doubters behind. Don't let anyone divert you from your future.
Journey on!

Insight #32

Your courage and strength are not always demonstrated by an explosive celebration or conquest. Sometimes it is simply reflected in the "next step" you have given yourself permission to take.
Journey on!

Worth

Insight #33

Gladly embrace your field of play. You are the coach and you are the player. It's not a spectator sport. You can't sit on the bench and watch. Play your game and give it everything you've got.

Journey on!

Insight #34

Honor is your reward for what you "give" in life, not for what you "receive." Give from your heart and soul and always receive in humility.

Journey on!

Insight #35

Always be the best "top notch" version of you rather than an imitation of someone else. You are the best you there will ever be!

Journey on!

Insight #36

Your dreams, passion, vision, and imagination will catapult you over any obstacle and any foe you encounter on your life's journey.

Journey on!

Genius

Insight #37

Learn to forgive others, for they are running in the same race as you—the Human Race. Everyone stumbles and falls at times. It's getting back up each time that matters.

Journey on!

Insight #38

When you give to others, do not dwell on what you have done. You will achieve and receive things you have never even imagined were possible.

Journey on!

Insight #39

Remember where your treasure lies—in your heart, your passion, and your love. Allow these gifts to guide you on your path.

Journey on!

Insight #40

Deal only with those you admire, respect, know, like, and trust. They will add to your strength, add energy, and not detract from it.

Journey on!

Embrace

Embrace

Just when the caterpillar
 thought the world was over
it became a butterfly.

RE Hollis

Insight #41

Daily reflection to enrich yourself will keep you focused on your directional beacon.

Journey on!

Insight #42

You always have enough to share and to give to others. All that you need comes from your God, and your spirit of sacrifice will move you forward.

Journey on!

Insight #43

You can do great things spiritually, personally, physically, mentally, and psychologically. Your hunger and thirst for that which is right will give you the direction and purpose you seek.

Journey on!

Insight #44

The level of discipline, motivation, strength, and purposeful actions required to achieve your goals and fulfill your destiny is a matter you must decide for yourself.

Journey on!

Uniqueness

Insight #45

External motivation is good, but it tends not to be lasting. That motivation, which comes from within, will cover your entire journey, remaining with you all the days of your life.

Journey on!

Insight #46

Your health and wholeness are dependent upon the decisions you make and the actions you choose to take. Choose well, for it is your future!

Journey on!

Insight #47

Whatever you vividly imagine, ardently desire, and enthusiastically act upon will eventually happen. Stay the course!

Journey on!

Insight #48

Doubts, frustrations, and setbacks are all normal. Your convictions, determination, values, and beliefs will provide the courage and perseverance to continue on.

Journey on!

Accomplishment

Insight #49

There are countless others you can turn to for guidance, support, and direction. Utilize those coaches and teachers to assist you in the decisions you must make.

Journey on!

Insight #50

Remember that each time you fall it is only a tragedy if you fail to rise up and continue in the direction of your "truth."

Journey on!

Insight #51

Live, love, laugh, play, dream, and reach for the stars as you journey on your road of life. It's a secret of the universe that few realize until it is too late. What will you do with your precious time?

Journey on!

Insight #52

A true master is never satisfied and never allows him or herself to become too comfortable. Stay your course, moving onward to your destiny.

Journey on!

Destiny

Insight #53

What will hold your focus of attention? That is, what shall determine your actions? Choose carefully, for it is your future.
Journey on!

Insight #54

The more you listen to people, the smarter they will think you are. Remember that one of the greatest courtesies you can extend to another individual is to listen to them.
Journey on!

Insight #55

Your time is such a precious commodity. Cherish it, for you have all the time there will ever be and there will never be any more of it. It is the time of your life.
Journey on!

Insight #56

You are as good as your next step. Properly plan each step to prevent poor decisions and poor performance and you will progress with confidence.
Journey on!

Celebrate

Insight #57

Count your blessings every day and do not dwell on misfortunes. Focus on that which energizes and strengthens you to carry on.

Journey on!

Insight #58

There will be crisis in your life. Count on it! However difficult, it's normal. Your vision, belief, hard work, and preparation will allow you to stay the course.

Journey on!

Insight #59

What are your expectations? That will become your reality for each day of your life. Expect the best!

Journey on!

Insight #60

Victory will be yours if you allow it to come into your life. Your beliefs, thoughts, energy, and every part of your being must embrace victory.

Journey on!

Courageous

Courageous

Worrying is like a rocking chair.
It gives you something to do,
but doesn't get you anywhere.

Insight #61

Remember when you thought winter would never end? More cold and storms always seemed to be on the way. The storms of your life will end and sunshine and warmth are about to break through.

Journey on!

Insight #62

Are you pursuing your dreams or are you creating the reality? As Ghandi said, "Be the change." Don't pretend. Be the "real self" you know you are and embrace your destiny.

Journey on!

Insight #63

Your giving and service to others is essential to a successful life. For this, you will receive your "right future." Remember, it's the giving, not the taking.

Journey on!

Insight #64

Each step you take today is forming your tomorrow. Move with dignity, grace, and appreciation that you are creating your future.

Journey on!

Give

Insight #65

You can't change the past, but the future can be a totally different story. Only you can begin that. Do it right now!
Journey on!

Insight #66

Don't just expect an abundant life filled with joy and wonder. Make it that way. Make it happen!
Journey on!

Insight #67

No matter what your age, your future awaits you. It is not too late to make those "might-have-beens" your reality.
Journey on!

Insight #68

Forgive people, obstacles, interruptions, and anything and anyone who distracted you or attempted to lead you astray from your destiny. Forgiveness is another essential ingredient you must possess in order to move forward.
Journey on!

Imagination

Insight #69

Your inner thoughts, enthusiasm, and attitude will reflect all that you display outwardly in your life. Change your inner being and you will be that person.

Journey on!

Insight #70

Love each step along the way. That is what truly makes the trip of our life worthwhile.

Journey on!

Insight #71

From your fears and stress will come some of the most worthwhile achievements and moments of your life. It's often difficult to see that at the time they occur, but realize that all things serve a purpose.

Journey on!

Insight #72

With each step you take on your Life's Journey, you are creating not only your "right future" but your "right self."

Journey on!

Achieve

Insight #73

Images, slogans, words of inspiration, and motivational quotes are all good tools of encouragement and support. However, only you can change these words into meaningful actions.

Journey on!

Insight #74

Your journey is like a puzzle containing thousands of pieces. With each step, a part of the picture comes together until you have clarity of understanding and can visualize your future.

Journey on!

Insight #75

Imitation is the highest form of flattery. Look to others for their best qualities, virtues, and take the best of the best to assist in your own unique formation.

Journey on!

Insight #76

It's not only the step you take, but the direction you step in that makes all the difference. Life as a result of this "can change" in an instance.

Journey on!

Admirable

Insight #77

Surround yourself with encouraging people who support and energize your hope and aspirations. That's the fuel you should fill your tank with, for it will propel you on the right path.

Journey on!

Insight #78

Don't do things half-heartedly. Be "all in!" Do whatever is right, necessary, proper, and just each and every time.

Journey on!

Insight #79

Before you can achieve your "big picture", you must paint and pay attention to the small strokes of the brush on the canvas of your life. Each one represents a step in the direction of your right future.

Journey on!

Insight #80

Can others count on you to allow yourself to move in the "right direction" through each daily action you take? Be the person you know and desire yourself to be.

Journey on!

Reflection

Reflection

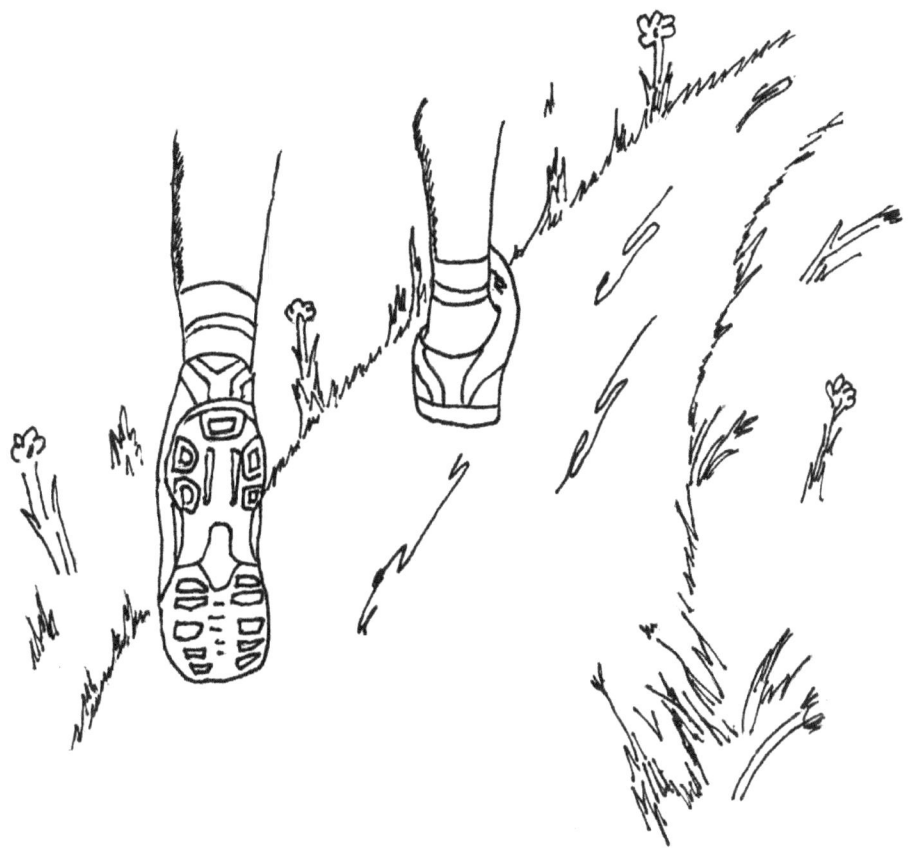

Each step forward gets you closer to your dream.

Insight #81

Pass the small tests by paying attention to that voice within you. It is there to assist in keeping you on the right path. No matter how small an item may be, they all add up to your "total package"—your future.

Journey on!

Insight #82

Excuses can keep you from your destiny. There should be no excuse that keeps you from moving in the direction of your right future. Always consider what actions you should take to replace and prevent an excuse from happening in the first place.

Journey on!

Insight #83

Everything counts! Big or small, they all play a role in your life. Don't confuse small with insignificant. They each lead to big things.

Journey on!

Insight #84

Focus on your "inner spirit", for that is where your real motivation lies. If it is taking place within, it will radiate outwardly to produce the results you desire.

Journey on!

Purpose

Insight #85

Your top priority must be you. You cannot assist others properly when you neglect "self". Being the best you allows you to manifest the confidence needed to stay the course.
Journey on!

Insight #86

Don't have defeat, fear, failure, or discouragement take root in your thoughts. Your thoughts should be only those that propel you in the direction of your destiny!
Journey on!

Insight #87

Be strong! Answer your challenges with the faith, confidence, values, and beliefs of your "inner spirit." When you allow that to radiate outwardly, you will continue to demonstrate that which will move you forward.
Journey on!

Insight #88

It's time to say "NO" to the good and "YES" to the great items that will truly take you to the next level. These are critical choices you must make and back up with your actions.
Journey on!

Motivation

Insight #89

What could have been? What should have been? Get over it! Give up all hope of a better past, learn from your experience, and move forward!

Journey on!

Insight #90

You will have doubts and concerns, but your inner spirit will provide the strength and determination to restore your faith and stay the course.

Journey on!

Insight #91

You may fail at times, but you are not a failure. Keep focused on your vision, your goals, and your destiny. That is where your success lies.

Journey on!

Insight #92

You are not a perfect being but a human being. Embrace your humanity and realize that each day you are not striving to be perfect but excellent.

Journey on!

Persevere

Insight #93

Today is the single most significant learning experience of your life—so far! But just wait for what is in front of you tomorrow!

Journey on!

Insight #94

Find something that no one else can do and then do it better than anybody else can do it. Then you will leave your mark on your life's journey.

Journey on!

Insight #95

"I give up!" "I don't care!" What message are you sending to your inner spirit when you speak such words? Stay the course! Live your vision!

Journey on!

Insight #96

Don't ever get too comfortable with where you are at. Your comfort lies with where you are going to. Your destiny!

Journey on!

Utilization

Insight #97

Be the person your inner spirit dreams to be. In so doing, you will create externally that individual you desire.
Journey on!

Insight #98

Today, may you find the strength, display the gratitude, demonstrate the kindness, and give of yourself to others. Those gifts you have been blessed to gather on each step of your journey.
Journey on!

Insight #99

Seek comfort in each step of your journey to nourish your inner spirit. Each step takes you closer to releasing that spirit as it creates your external self. Your future and your destiny awaits you.
Journey on!

Insight #100

Freely bring and share your gifts, talents, and skills with others. Only you possess the ability to grant permission for this to happen. You will prosper as a result of your giving.
Journey on!

Satisfaction

Satisfaction

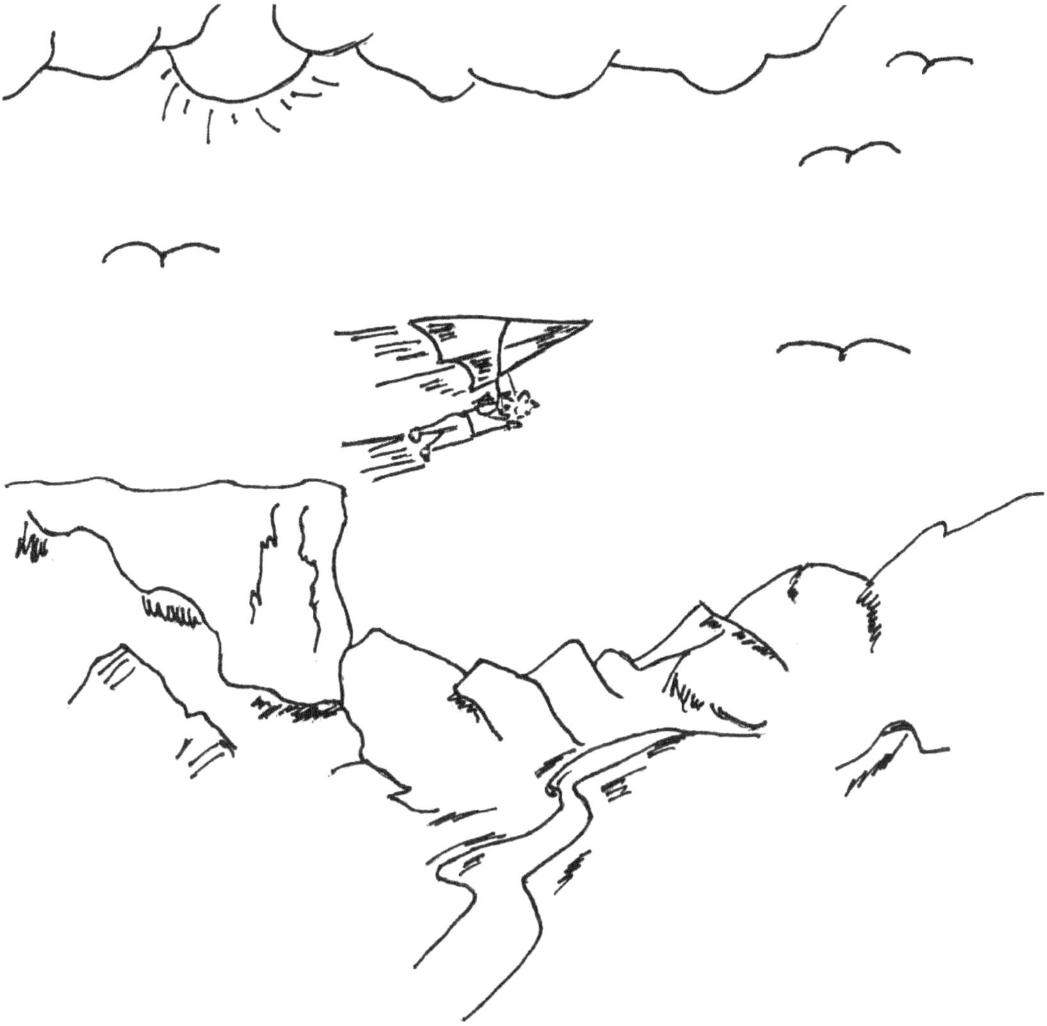

Soar with the eagles to become
the best "you" there is.

RE Hollis

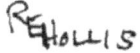

Awareness Promotes Effectiveness
There are Always Alternatives to Consider

There are always alternatives to consider—think! You are in control if you so choose to be!

You will encounter so much on your journey. What an incredible learning experience it is. Remember (and this is one of the most challenging items for many to accept and embrace) that you are inescapably responsible for your own actions and the consequences of those actions. Once you accept that, you are on your way because now you are accountable for you! You are in charge! You are in control. Action, destiny, future, goals, wants, needs, desires, wins, losses, success and failure—you accept it all and you learn from it. THAT IS SO POWERFUL!

That gives you the power!
To confront the challenges before you!
To keep you going!
To move forward!
To face your reality!

The power:
> To embrace your destiny!
> To learn from your failures!
> To evolve and grow daily!
> To embrace your humanity!
> To keep on keeping on!

The power:
> To try and try and try!
> Recognize your full potential!
> To achieve that breakthrough!
> To achieve a flood of abundance!

The power:
> To know you will succeed!
> To change your life forever!
> To understand the value in all that life presents to you!
> To recognize and embrace the genius of others!

The power:
- To be committed to your goals!
- To be committed to your values!
- To identify where you are!
- To identify where you want to be!

The power:
- To learn from each step you take!
- To embrace your truth!
- To maintain your focus!
- To own your reality!

The power:
- To deal with the fact of life!
- To have one breakthrough after another!
- To go to higher levels than you ever imagined!

From all of this you will acquire and embrace:
- Humility.
- A thirst for knowledge.
- Gratefulness and gratitude.
- Realization of the significance of others.
- My humanity.
- The ability to accept my failures and learning from them.
- The ability to confront my challenges.
- Experience growth and change.
- The value and genius of each individual.
- Confront your problems.

Your failures will no longer hold you down because you will see them as learning opportunities. Forgive yourself. You do not need to suffer with your mistakes. Trust yourself and move on!

Insight #101

Don't look back, for you are not going in that direction. Look forward—to your destiny!

Journey on!

Insight #102

Why travel with those who do not share or support or believe in your vision? Surround yourself with those who will energize and propel you forward!

Journey on!

Insight #103

Will the pace change throughout your journey? Absolutely! There are times to move it up a notch; rise to a challenge. There are times to slow it down and take it all in. Your willingness to adjust and adapt to a situation, to people, and to your environment is reflected in your caring, your passion, and your actions.

Journey on!

Insight #104

What is your game plan? Your vision, mission, and strategic objectives—your goals—are all interdependently related. They are intended to support and complement each other while pointing you in the direction of your future.

Journey on!

Courtesy

Insight #105

Your journey is not a spectator sport. Get involved! Participate in your life. Imagine it, dream it, and make it happen! Play the game of your life!

Journey on!

Insight #106

Every morning and evening, use imagery to capture your vision and confirm your direction. Read to work on your inner spirit and enhance your skills. Then deliver through your outward actions.

Journey on!

Insight #107

Keep a journal. Write down your thoughts, hopes, and aspirations. Your writing will encourage your reading. Your reading will assist in leading. Write to lead and read to lead!

Journey on!

Insight #108

There are times when you must re-energize. Use your MAP (Make A Plan), chart your course, prepare your route, and you are back on the move!

Journey on!

Plan

Insight #109

Celebrate your success! It builds confidence and creates a thirst for more!

Journey on!

Insight #110

Get out of your comfort zone. Stretch and reach beyond the known to the unknown. You will grow to heights you never imagined.

Journey on!

Insight #111

You may choose to lose unless at first you win from within. Let your inner spirit guide you.

Journey on!

Insight #112

Your destiny will not just happen. Maximize the transition from where you are to where you desire to be. Work for it! Make it happen! It is your future!

Journey on!

Vision

Insight #113

First you must come into complete agreement with yourself psychologically, personally, and emotionally. Then you can give yourself permission to move forward without resistance. You now have complete buy-in with self and now can externalize the appropriate actions to produce the desires of your inner spirit.

Journey on!

Insight #114

If you don't like what you are doing, saying, or if the actions you demonstrate do not produce the results you desire, change by asking the key questions to clarify your inner spirit. Then the changes will come forth from your core being.

Journey on!

Insight #115

Confusion, distortion, and frustration are the result of a misdirected inner spirit. Before you can reach out with meaningful, solid, clear actions with confidence, you must first listen to your inner being.

Journey on!

Insight #116

Feed your inner spirit and your external being will reflect that inner beauty. It will lift you up to that next level of achievement and excellence.

Journey on!

Victory

Insight #117

Keeping your sights on your vision and your goals will keep all the challenges and obstacles under your feet as you step forward!

Journey on!

Insight #118

All your struggles and pain will dwindle as you look to where you are going, not to where you have been. Your future awaits you!

Journey on!

Insight #119

Those against you will falter and fall by the wayside as you boldly tread on each task before you.

Journey on!

Insight #120

Your faith, values, and beliefs will keep you on your course to your destiny. Believe it and do it! It is your reality, your future.

Journey on!

Transcend

Transcend

Seed your life's journey with excellence, positive thoughts, perseverance, and personal values.

RE Hollis

Insight #121

Do whatever is right, necessary, proper, and just and no one will dare to stand in your way or distract you from your chosen course of action.

Journey on!

Insight #122

The one place where you will lose your challenge is in your own mind. Your perception, your attitude, determination, and stick-to-itiveness are critical. Clothe yourself with a passion that will propel you forward to victory!

Journey on!

Insight #123

You are equipped for those whatever life will confront you with. However, it's up to you to put those essential items into operation. Only you can be the "driver" on your journey.

Journey on!

Insight #124

No one can change your attitude, alter your course, or stop your progress without your permission. Continue on and stay on that high road you have chosen. It is your right future!

Journey on!

Grace

Insight #125

Don't just be in pursuit of your "right future," create it!
Journey on!

Insight #126

Keep your vision in front of you. That's the direction you want to keep moving in!
Journey on!

Insight #127

We have a small model sailboat and on the main sail is our version of Archimedes holding a staff in order to move the world. It is a constant reminder to "Find Your Place to Stand and Build the Right Future." What is your constant reminder?
Journey on!

Insight #128

You keep moving toward what you consistently believe in, have a vision of, and value. By doing that, it will embed itself in your inner spirit and radiate outward.
Journey on!

Abundance

Insight #129

What do you think about? What do you dwell on and desire? That is where you are heading. That is the future you are creating.

Journey on!

Insight #130

Our vision is to reach out to millions of people around the world to help them in creating their own right future while having a purposeful journey. What is your vision?

Journey on!

Insight #131

What do you vividly imagine? That is the true beginning of fulfilling your destiny. Dream it, believe it, and then take action!

Journey on!

Insight #132

Keep your goals, your vision, your destiny out in front of you as a constant reminder. That serves as your directional beacon, guiding you to your right future.

Journey on!

Forgiveness

Insight #133

What is your proverbial carrot that you have dangling in front of you to keep you reaching, stretching, and moving forward? It constantly reminds you of what you will become, do, and make a part of your life. It gives you a purposeful journey.

Journey on!

Insight #134

Are you concentrating on past failures, disappointments, and problems or are you focused on where you are going? Your future awaits you.

Journey on!

Insight #135

Shake off your doubt and frustrations. Stop pushing yourself down and start pushing yourself forward.

Journey on!

Insight #136

The ability to continually restore and refuel your inner spirit and stay on your chosen course rests with you and your resolve to keep your faith in all that you hold precious. Your ideals, values, and the very principles you live by will be tested daily. Have you built a firm foundation that will withstand the stresses and strains your journey will present you with? You have!

Journey on!

Attitude

Insight #137

It is said that anger does more harm to the vessel in which it is stored than to the object upon which it is poured. Deal with your anger before it takes you off your course and conquers you. Anger is not something that must happen. It is something you choose to allow to happen. It's your choice!

Journey on!

Insight #138

What has gotten a hold of you? Is it those things that pull you down, tear you apart emotionally and psychologically, or that which lifts you up and moves you along your path with confidence, conviction, and determination? It's your choice as to what you will allow your inner spirit to embrace.

Journey on!

Insight #139

Getting involved, taking action, and making every day count will only be empty words to fill empty pages if you do not pick up your pen and write your story. It is dependent upon your ability to give yourself permission to act! Only you can write the story of your life, which desperately needs to be told.

Journey on!

Insight #140

It does matter where you are going, who you are walking with, what you are reading, the positive uplifting and supportive people and experiences you feed your inner spirit with. It all matters! Choose wisely.

Journey on!

Performance

Performance

You can't change the direction of the wind, but you can adjust your sails.

RE Hollis

Insight #141

Are you in agreement with your actions? Are you expressing mediocrity and expecting greatness? It won't happen. Talk the walk!

Journey on!

Insight #142

You have everything you require to take your journey with the exception of one critical element—your permission to allow yourself to fulfill your destiny. Only you can do that!

Journey on!

Insight #143

Getting involved, taking action, and making every day count will only be empty words to fill empty pages if you do not pick up your pen and write your story. It is dependent upon your ability to give yourself permission to act! Only you can write the story of your life, which desperately needs to be told.

Journey on!

Insight #144

It does matter where you are going, who you are walking with, what you are reading, the positive uplifting and supportive people and experiences you feed your inner spirit with. It all matters! Choose wisely.

Journey on!

Support

Insight #145

You need time to relax, to reflect, and to sharpen your saw. Strive for a balance in your life.

Journey on!

Insight #146

Joy and discovery await you at the end of your journey. There is no obstacle or person you should fear as you reach for your destiny.

Journey on!

Insight #147

Be the person you dream to be. By doing so, you will create that right future you strive for.

Journey on!

Insight #148

Do not doubt the path you are on to your destiny. You are creating your future with each step you take.

Journey on!

Virtue

Insight #149

Today, may I have the strength, display the gratitude, demonstrate the kindness, and give to others those gifts I have been blessed to gather with each step of my journey.
Journey on!

Insight #150

You have a dream in your heart and spirit. Hold firm and stay your course. You are creating your own right future.
Journey on!

Insight #151

Hostility, anger, and bitterness are the result of an unforgiving spirit. Do not harbor such things in your heart.
Journey on!

Insight #152

Get your thoughts going in the right direction. They will propel you forward to your destiny!
Journey on!

Surround

Insight #153

FOCUS—Focus on your One charted Course Until you are Successful! Don't underestimate the power of concentration.
Journey on!

Insight #154

Don't become a victim of "If only…" statements. If only I were stronger. If only I were younger. If only I had a better job. If only… They are excuses that stop you from moving forward.
Journey on!

Insight #155

You must be able to look beyond what others see and beyond the surface. Discover your incredible value and genius. Get rid of those condemning thoughts that prevent you from realizing your potential.
Journey on!

Insight #156

You will be asked to do challenging things in your life. As you travel along your path, much will be revealed. Be in agreement with your inner spirit and move forward with conviction.
Journey on!

Attention

Insight #157

Are you willing to sacrifice to attain your destiny? You will be tested. Trust, believe, and hold firm to your convictions.
Journey on!

Insight #158

Difficult situations will present themselves. You will be confronted with challenges and you will often wonder how will this all work out? Stay the course. You will persevere!
Journey on!

Insight #159

Meditate and reflect each morning on where you are going that day to determine your own destiny. Meditate and reflect each evening on what you have done that moved you along your path to the future. It keeps you focused and on track.
Journey on!

Insight #160

Wonderful things are coming your way. Are you ready to be receptive to growth, change, and moving in the direction of your destiny?
Journey on!

Direction

1,000 Ways in 1,000 Days to Win from Within!

Direction

Insight #161

It's easy to get stuck in a rut during your journey. Your perseverance and determination will thrust you forward so that you can continue.

Journey on!

Insight #162

Stay away from those who pull you down, who do not believe in you, who do not invest in you, and those who attempt to feed you "can't-do thoughts." Surround yourself with people who move you forward.

Journey on!

Insight #163

You are meant to move to a higher level with each step you take as you move forward. The key is that you must take that first step, then another, and so forth.

Journey on!

Insight #164

You must have an uncommon belief that you hold firm to. It is the rudder of your boat directing your path. The sails you set will move you along your chosen course.

Journey on!

Spirit

Insight #165

Your life will follow your thoughts. If you think all hope is gone, it is! If you believe you will not succeed, you won't! If you think failure, you will fail! What thoughts do you promote to move you forward? Think, expect, and believe the best. It will happen!
Journey on!

Insight #166

A victorious life will be yours if you do not just say "the pledge" but live it! "This is my Life's Journey. I am the only one who can chart my course. My decisions and my actions will determine my direction and my final destination. I will find my place to stand and build my right future."
Journey on!

Insight #167

Like a river that overflows its banks, your life of goodness will overflow the path you walk and affect others in a positive, uplifting manner.
Journey on!

Insight #168

Remember, what you think and speak is predictive of your future. What are you creating? Is it a declaration of doom or a call to success and prosperity? Be the future you desire in word and deed and you will create it!
Journey on!

Propel

Insight #169

You may not know it just yet, but you are creating your own destiny. Your victory awaits you if you stay the course. You will receive and achieve the future your actions are calling for.
Journey on!

Insight #170

You are unique, confident, courageous, and able to move forward with class, charisma, style, grace, and determination. Accept your destiny. Answer the call to your right future!
Journey on!

Insight #171

What do I really care about? What is best for me? Let me see the light that I need to follow so that I am on the right course to create my right future.
Journey on!

Insight #172

If you are talking about losing and defeat, count on it! If you are speaking victory and success, count on it!
Journey on!

Value

Insight #173

The more you speak of losing or being a victim, frustrated or depressed, tired and ill, the more you are creating that future for yourself. Speak of winning, victory, accomplishment and joy, energy and health. Make that your destiny.

Journey on!

Insight #174

You have been to the edge of defeat, about to fail and take a fall. However, you will not go over that edge but climb to the next level. You are not going to fall but fly and soar to new success. Stay the course!

Journey on!

Insight #175

When you speak out loud and declare your positive intentions, you are releasing your inner spirit and promoting your own success.

Journey on!

Insight #176

Look for the genius in every person and you will find it. It is there and if you hold fast, you will discover even more than expected.

Journey on!

Determination

Insight #177

Just like a plant that does not have its roots nourished and withers away, we too may wither if we do not feed our inner spirit. Feel victory and expect success. Declare health, class, excellence, charm, positive growth, and that will be your future.
Journey on!

Insight #178

You are well able to accomplish your desired future. Choose it, believe it, speak it, do it, and achieve it! It's your choice!
Journey on!

Insight #179

Look at the obstacles before you and speak to them. Announce your intentions of crossing the bridges, climbing the hills, and making your way as you carve out a "right" future.
Journey on!

Insight #180

When you surround yourself with those who uplift you and encourage your dreams, you are providing new energy at each turn in the road of your Life's Journey.
Journey on!

Humanity

Humanity

There is no elevator to success.
You have to take the stairs.

Insight #181

Don't just talk to be heard. Gather and share wisdom that will give you and others confidence, assurance, strength, and boldness to stay the course.

Journey on!

Insight #182

What is the anchor in your life, that which provides security, a directional beacon that keeps you on course not only when there is smooth sailing, but through the storms?

Journey on!

Insight #183

Others will attempt to lessen your importance by no support, encouragement, or adding to your movement in the direction of your destiny. Your passion and belief in your purpose will lift you up and move you forward.

Journey on!

Insight #184

Be true to yourself and who you are. That is where your real strength and uniqueness lies. Capitalize upon those talents and use them to propel yourself forward.

Journey on!

Significant

Insight #185

The plan for your life is in place. However, you must live it and permit it to happen. It's your choice to embrace your destiny or to take another path.

Journey on!

Insight #186

When it is all said and done, you will achieve your destiny. Your future will appear as a result of your sincere effort's determination.

Journey on!

Insight #187

Choose your battles well. They take time and energy to fight. Fight those battles that will result in moving you forward. The others do not deserve your attention.

Journey on!

Insight #188

It takes courage to stand strong in your truth. Utilize your gifts and talents to support your beliefs and fix whatever it is that is presenting itself as a challenge.

Journey on!

Comfort

Insight #189

Each day, know that you have given it your all. You will sleep very well and be ready to repeat the process the next day.
Journey on!

Insight #190

You know what actions you must take to accomplish the tasks before you. Use your ingenuity and permission to get the job done!
Journey on!

Insight #191

Your enthusiasm will permit you to fail and carry on, to fail and carry on, and to fail and carry on to eventual success.
Journey on!

Insight #192

Your experiences are learning tools. Now take those tools and build your future.
Journey on!

Kindness

Insight #193

Treat others according to your expectations of them and they will inevitably live up to those expectations. Be certain to live up to your own expectations.

Journey on!

Insight #194

Don't mourn for your past but live and embrace your present and create the right future.

Journey on!

Insight #195

Question your way to success. Be certain to listen and grow from the answers.

Journey on!

Insight #196

Challenge yourself to love someone you often have difficulties with. Somewhere inside of them lies their genius and it will amaze you.

Journey on!

Permission

Insight #197

Look for service from others as little as possible and look to serve others as much as possible. As you give, so shall you receive.

Journey on!

Insight #198

With each success you encounter, move on to the next success and then the next and the next and the next…

Journey on!

Insight #199

What have you found that you have a passion for and are willing to die for so that you may live and endure whatever life presents to you?

Journey on!

Insight #200

You will alter your life when you alter your inner spirit. That attitude will transition your thoughts into action.

Journey on!

Forward

Forward

Awareness Promotes Effectiveness

Dreams and Goals All Begin from Within!

Dreams and goals all begin from within. That's the prerequisite for it to flourish. This is where you learn to trust yourself. Your moves are the direction you will chart and follow. From within they will radiate forth the abundance of your dreams. This is where you are forged as steel to be firm and bold and aligned with your values, beliefs, and convictions.

This is not always a comfortable situation. It may produce great stress and turmoil, but it is a time of preparation. This is where you are being fine-tuned, sharpened, and arriving at a realization of what truly lies ahead and you will move forward with confidence. Until you pass through such a storm you will not find the light of your destiny, your future.

You do not always comprehend each pit, twist, and turn you will travel in your journey. However, with each step, you are moving forward, you are learning and gathering strength, knowledge, and skills to accomplish and fulfill your purpose. You know the road will level off, straighten out, and there will be smooth sailing. It is up to you to carry on, move forward, and not give up or give in.

When you embrace this thinking, you will cease the wishing and a hoping, you will stop whining and making excuses, you will expect abundance, and you will live up to those expectations you have established and set forth for yourself.

Stop feeding your inner spirit with "if only" statements:

    If only I was bigger and stronger, then I could make a difference.
    If only I was younger
    If only I was older
    If only I had more education
    If only I was in a wonderful relationship
    If only, if only, if only…

You are burying yourself with this type of an attitude and you are setting yourself up for disappointment and failure.

Set your expectations high and allow yourself to live up to them.

Insight #201

You will have to be brave to forgive those who divert you along your journey. You must be brave to stay the course.
Journey on!

Insight #202

There are things before you which you think you cannot do. Those are the very things you must and will do to move forward.
Journey on!

Insight #203

Change is not easy but necessary to restructure, reposition, and reinvent yourself in order to survive and thrive. Ah! It's a secret of the YOUniverse.
Journey on!

Insight #204

You have a tremendous influence over other people's lives. You must acquire discipline in order to maintain and control that discipline to be effective.
Journey on!

Goals

Insight #205

In a sense, your future cannot wait. It is counting on you to move closer each day as you make and create a portion of that future.

Journey on!

Insight #206

Your voice needs to be heard. Your actions need to be taken. Together, they will change your world.

Journey on!

Insight #207

Don't look for mistakes, flaws, failures, and setbacks, for you will find them. Look for remedies, cures, achievements, and solutions. They are waiting for your discovery.

Journey on!

Insight #208

Hope begins during some of your darkest moments. All seems at a loss; you are confused and stumbling when suddenly comes the dawn showing you the way.

Journey on!

Participate

Insight #209

All the love and passion you give to a cause is never lost. Even in failure, it will flow back to you giving rejuvenation and strength to carry on.

Journey on!

Insight #210

That project, task, and goal you have set for yourself will simply not work unless you do! Give yourself permission to act and turn those dreams into realities.

Journey on!

Insight #211

You may not know exactly what your future holds in store for you, but realize and know that you hold your future. You are the key; you are the deciding factor to make it all happen!

Journey on!

Insight #212

Your freedom to unleash your own future rests in your ability to allow yourself to boldly go where you have not gone before.

Journey on!

Lead

Insight #213

There are so many challenges, opponents, and obstacles you can conquer with love. Your heart power is the real strength you possess to drive your passion for success.
Journey on!

Insight #214

If you do not believe in yourself, how do you expect others to believe in you? When you make a plan and chart your course of action, your knowledge and love of self will nurture that belief.
Journey on!

Insight #215

Courage and strength come from giving freely from the heart and receiving graciously from others.
Journey on!

Insight #216

New worlds will open for you with each new experience you encounter, each new friend you meet, and every obstacle you confront.
Journey on!

Stretch

Insight #217

If you do not have plan or a sense of the direction you are going in, any path will get you to the land of confusion and disappointment. Chart your course and set your sails for your chosen port.

Journey on!

Insight #218

Every step you take is a touchstone of the dreams you are turning into realities. Trust in your ability to create a journey you will rejoice in every day of your life.

Journey on!

Insight #219

All the obstacles and challenges you will confront will not be able to be changed, but none of them will even begin to change until you confront them.

Journey on!

Insight #220

Your passion for life will give you the courage to believe in even the impossible and will move you forward beyond your imagination.

Journey on!

Win

Win

Don't let FEAR impede your Life's Journey.

False
Expectations
Appearing
Real

Insight #221

With each step you take, you will find your place to stand if each step is grounded in responsibility for your own actions.
Journey on!

Insight #222

Your love can be shared, divided, given away, and will not diminish. For as you give, it is replenished and multiplied many times over by your inner spirit.
Journey on!

Insight #223

Each step you begin to take today will lead you to your tomorrow and on to your right future.
Journey on!

Insight #224

You will discover that as you are driven by your passion until it hurts, eventually the hurt will diminish and you will find even more passion.
Journey on!

Appropriate

Insight #225

Do not overvalue and overestimate what you are not. It causes you to undervalue and underestimate what you really are. You are a person of value and genius.

Journey on!

Insight #226

Be a positive and supportive individual unto yourself in your spoken word or be quiet. You cannot speak defeat and expect victory.

Journey on!

Insight #227

There are no limits to what can be accomplished other than the limits you set for yourself.

Journey on!

Insight #228

We use devices such as rulers to measure. Are you measuring up to the challenges you have accepted? Don't let yourself down.

Journey on!

Meaningful

Insight #229

You will never quite achieve perfection, but you should always strive for it while achieving excellence.

Journey on!

Insight #230

Be careful not to overvalue what you are not while undervaluing all that you are. You are a unique creation of the YOUniverse.

Journey on!

Insight #231

Your positive attitude and your example should be infectious to others.

Journey on!

Insight #232

Your experience is of great value and grows exponentially with each step along your path.

Journey on!

Future

Insight #233

Fate will bring you together with people you never even imagined. Rejoice with all your heart for the genius to be discovered within each of them.

Journey on!

Insight #234

Do not let your heart ever harden, for it will divert you from your path and close your mind to the beauty of life.

Journey on!

Insight #235

When you give up all hope of a better past, you are refusing to allow yesterday to take away your focus on today.

Journey on!

Insight #236

Your time is such a precious item and once used, can never be recaptured. Use your time wisely, for it is where your future is created.

Journey on!

Belief

Insight #237

Take a mindful walk each day. It is a wonderful time to feed your inner spirit with words of strength, courage, and commitment.
Journey on!

Insight #238

It should not matter who (if anyone) is watching or listening when it comes to your values, ideals, and faith. They should remain consistent throughout your journey.
Journey on!

Insight #239

If you want to open the floodgates of happiness, Love is the answer!
Journey on!

Insight #240

From time to time as you travel your path, reach back and bring someone forward with you. It is an exercise in caring and love. It will strengthen your heart.
Journey on!

Perception

Perception

The moment you want to quit is the moment you want to keep pushing.

Be the best YOU you can be!

RE Hollis

Insight #241

Even a negative is not always a negative. It may just be the tipping point, opportunity, or stimulus required to charting your course of action.

Journey on!

Insight #242

You are like an active volcano, a tornadic wind, a hurricane in perfect power. Properly position and focus yourself to unleash your energy.

Journey on!

Insight #243

When you fall, fall forward, not back. When you fail, fail up, not down. Your movement should always be in the direction of your destiny.

Journey on!

Insight #244

Your true potential for greatness rests within you. Only you hold the key to unleashing your genius.

Journey on!

Equipped

Insight #245

Remember that at times some small, almost undetectable act on your part, may be the catalyst to change another's life forever.

Journey on!

Insight #246

Turn your face to your future for that is where you are going. Your past falls behind you.

Journey on!

Insight #247

Wonderful things are coming to you. Are you prepared to be receptive to growth, progress, prosperity, and moving in the right direction of your destiny?

Journey on!

Insight #248

Get involved! Don't be satisfied with just skimming the surface. Like the ocean, there is so much more below. Go deep! Big challenges will present you with big problems, calling upon you for big results. Go deep!

Journey on!

Pursuit

Insight #249

You are not ordinary but extraordinary! You are an amazing individual, so be prepared for the amazing challenges before you. Let your genius come forth!

Journey on!

Insight #250

You are shaped and fashioned with each step you take toward your destiny. That reflects your passion, your spirit, and all that you love and hold dear.

Journey on!

Insight #251

Reflect back periodically on the path you have already traveled. It all counts! The good and the bad. It has all served a purpose in shaping you into the unique individual you are today. You know what items to repeat and enhance and you now realize what must be avoided. Learn and prosper!

Journey on!

Insight #252

Many will find fault with you and not everyone will like you. Stay your course, for your destiny will provide the means to take care of those you must confront.

Journey on!

Radiate

Insight #253

The simplest form of gratitude is the joy you express with those who have assisted you on your journey.
Journey on!

Insight #254

Where is your focus? Are you concentrating on your struggles, disappointments, defeats, and failures, or will you focus on the positives—your victories, opportunities, the increase and abundance that you are going to receive.
Journey on!

Insight #255

Prepare for liftoff! Each morning, announce to yourself that "good things are going to take place." That is your launch pad to prosperity. Think it, believe it, and do it!
Journey on!

Insight #256

You have an incredible advantage every day. It's you! You are one of a kind and the only one who can create that right future. What an opportunity lies before you!
Journey on!

Desire

Insight #257

When you are charting your course, use your head—think first, then move forward with confidence. When you are dealing with others, remember to use your heart.
Journey on!

Insight #258

Someone once said to another, "You have such a 'Peter Pan heart'." What a wonderful compliment. Don't ever lose your childlike heart, for there lies purity and kindness.
Journey on!

Insight #259

Favor awaits you! This is your moment in time. Awaken and allow your inner spirit to move you forward and achieve your destiny.
Journey on!

Insight #260

Opposition is not all bad. At times, it is just the catalyst needed to ignite your fire! A kite rises against the wind and reaches great heights due to that opposing force.
Journey on!

Serve

Serve

Don't expect anyone else
to make you successful;
it's a do-it-yourself project.

RE Hollis

Insight #261

Yes, there are times when you will feel overwhelmed, frustrated, saddened, and even fearful. You will endure the storms of your life. The set of your sails will propel you along your charted course to your right future.

Journey on!

Insight #262

When you are closest to victory, you will often confront your greatest challenge. This is the time to call upon your inner spirit for the strength to push forward.

Journey on!

Insight #263

Giving is not something you have to do. It is not so much a duty that is assigned. It should be embraced as a privilege and a blessing.

Journey on!

Insight #264

An abundance of promotion is in your future. You will be elevated to heights you have never even imagined. You must persevere and not quit.

Journey on!

Proverbial

Insight #265

You do not have to be the fastest in this race, but you must keep on running. With each step, continue your forward movement to your future.

Journey on!

Insight #266

Yes, journal each day, but also write it in your heart and embrace it. Live it so that each day is the greatest day of your life—so far!

Journey on!

Insight #267

Your past does not define you, but it does prepare you! You learn from each success and even the failures encountered along your journey.

Journey on!

Insight #268

When something doesn't go as you expected, do not dwell upon it for such a period of time that you miss the next opportunity that presents itself. Stay focused on what lies ahead.

Journey on!

Restore

Insight #269

If you can assist another in the discovery of their own genius, you have done a very noble thing.
Journey on!

Insight #270

Have a grand vision, a noble cause, and a magnificent obsession, for you are destined to become what you believe.
Journey on!

Insight #271

One of the greatest courtesies we can extend to another human being is to listen to them.
Journey on!

Insight #272

You will confront many distractions from negativity, critics, and those who do not support or believe in your desires or your vision. You may even be attacked. Trust your heart and continue to move forward on your path.
Journey on!

Conviction

Insight #273

May you be part of a cause that is greater than yourself. It will add to your growth and wholeness as an individual.

Journey on!

Insight #274

Remember that your destination is the result of each small step you have taken to reach that end place. Your destiny is the result of each and every small task you have accomplished, and only when combined together do they equal the greatness you have achieved.

Journey on!

Insight #275

You've got what it takes! Believe and have confidence in your ability. Then, follow through with the firmness of your convictions to make it happen!

Journey on!

Insight #276

Others are not traveling your exact path—you are! Stay the course, for it reflects your values, beliefs, dreams, and aspirations.

Journey on!

Uplifting

Insight #277

If you truly want to be prepared for all the possible changes life will offer, practice humility.

Journey on!

Insight #278

Your inner spirit develops your dreams, your hopes, and desires. When you allow that inner spirit to radiate outward, you are awakening and bringing those items to life.

Journey on!

Insight #279

Be selective in the challenges you take on and the battles you fight. Do what matters in fulfilling your destiny and stay your course.

Journey on!

Insight #280

Once you have discovered your passion, pursue it relentlessly. Have a complete and total focus upon it and utilize your whole heart and being.

Journey on!

Fulfill

Fulfill

"Bridging the gap from where you are to where you want to be."

RE Hollis

Insight #281

There are consequences for your actions when you step forward in the direction of your destiny and when you step off your chosen path. You are responsible for the choices you make.

Journey on!

Insight #282

Do what you know you are supposed to do. Listen to your inner spirit. Trust and have faith in that inner voice that is driving you on.

Journey on!

Insight #283

Be bold in your actions. Don't wait. Don't hesitate. Go with your heart while supporting your actions with your mind. Take that step forward to your future.

Journey on!

Insight #284

Your future is waiting on you. Will you step forward to embrace it? Each step takes you there, but each step requires your permission to move ahead.

Journey on!

Voyage

Insight #285

I am going to move forward no matter what the circumstances, for I know my destiny, and it is my future. No obstacle shall divert or prevent me from taking the action I know I must take.
Journey on!

Insight #286

You will never be the same as you travel your path. With each forward motion, a new you is emerging to embrace your future.
Journey on!

Insight #287

Your focus all along has been on your own personal growth and development so you are best able to serve others. It begins with you, but knows no limitations!
Journey on!

Insight #288

By giving to others, you are advancing yourself on your own journey. Others will lift you up to the pinnacle of success through those very efforts of assisting them along the way.
Journey on!

Strive

Insight #289

Your Life's Journey will be extraordinary when you stay your course and remain true to your values.

Journey on!

Insight #290

Feed your inner spirit by allowing the good, positive, uplifting, high quality, high levels of readings, presentations, and inspirations to enter into your heart. Only you hold the key to open that door.

Journey on!

Insight #291

We so often say that "it's all about you," but that is only so that through your own achievements, development, skills, and knowledge you are in a better position to give, serve, and assist others.

Journey on!

Insight #292

Do not be so righteous that you blind yourself to the truth that is bigger than all of us. We are here to assist each other and grow together.

Journey on!

Dream

Insight #293

You may have walked with greatness and never knew it. Do not be quick to judge. Don't judge by the exterior of a person. You do not understand how they are feeding their inner spirit, which may be as bright as the sun and just about to radiate forth.

Journey on!

Insight #294

Remember that you are on the journey of your life. You are not a finished product. You are growing with each step.

Journey on!

Insight #295

What is the condition of your heart? Love is the key! Only you can open your heart to the love required to feed your inner spirit.

Journey on!

Insight #296

Remember (and this is one of the most challenging items for many to accept and embrace) that you are inescapably responsible for your own actions and the consequences of those actions. Once you accept responsibility, you are on your way because now you are accountable for you! You are in charge! You are in control!

Journey on!

Blessed

Insight #297

To step forward requires a conscious effort and focus of attention on your part. If your focus is on the past and you are not letting the past go, you will not move forward.
Journey on!

Insight #298

You can be discouraged, angry, frustrated, and down for the rest of your life if you allow it, and you are preventing yourself from your destiny. It's your choice to keep looking backward or to move forward.
Journey on!

Insight #299

Sadness is normal, but to cling to sadness and live with sadness your entire life is not. The rest of your life awaits you. Won't you make the journey? There are so many beautiful things that lie ahead. Embrace your future!
Journey on!

Insight #300

The past is past. It is over and done. The future is bright, alive, and glowing. It needs you. Your future begins today! Look forward, move forward, and step forward.
Journey on!

Heartfelt

Heartfelt

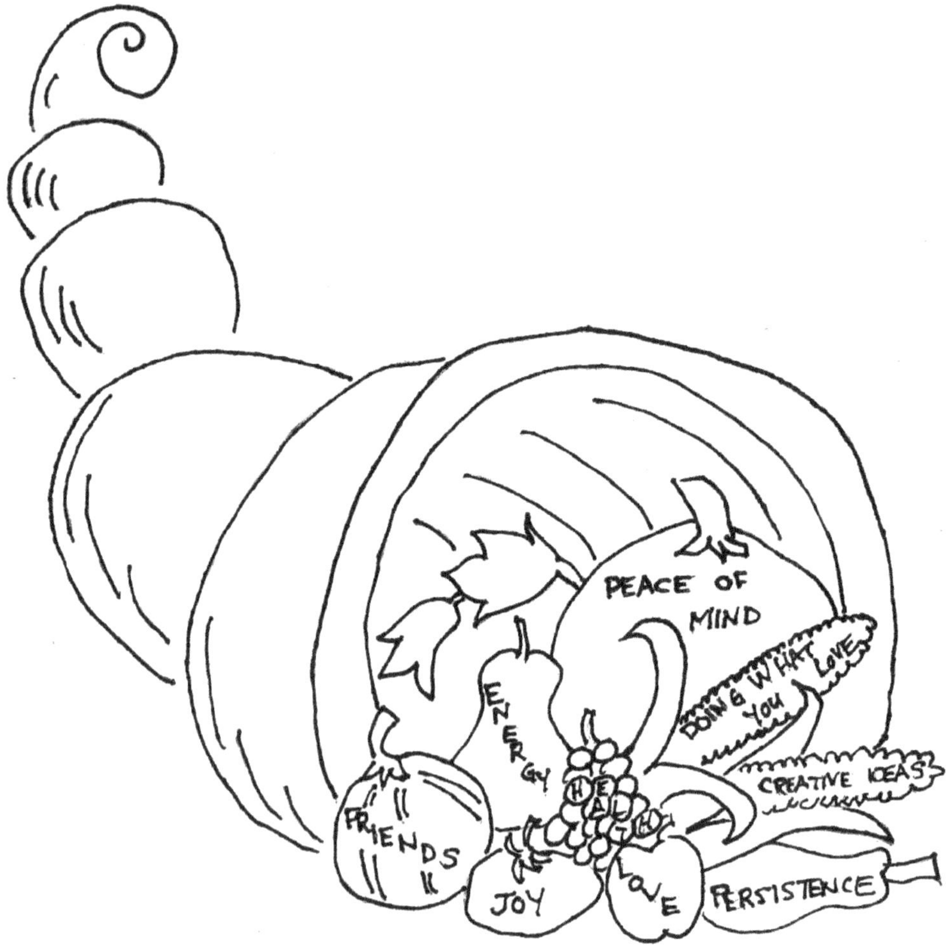

Abundance is what happens when we reflect on our blessings and not on our misfortunes.

RE HOLLIS

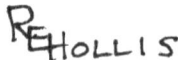

Awareness Promotes Effectiveness

Be a Gentle Soul

Be a gentle soul
as you travel at the speed of life.
Be a caring soul
to those you encounter along your journey.
Be a giving soul
as you cross paths with the genius of each individual.
Be a spirited soul
as you radiate outward that which is born within.
Be an imaginative soul
as you create your own right future.
Be a committed soul
as you have a purposeful journey.

You are the right person, at the right time,
in the right place, for the right reasons,
doing the right things.
You are set up for success and victory.

The critical factor is your ability
to give yourself permission to
take action and move forward.

To be responsible and accountable
for your own actions while accepting
The consequences that go along with that.

When you truly know yourself, your values,
purpose, vision, and goals, then making
such decisions with confidence and determination
becomes almost second nature. Be your own catalyst.
That driving force from within that says,
"Yes, I can!" "Yes, I will!"

Insight #301

The first place you will lose a battle, a life's challenge, or a task is within your inner being. If you believe you are beaten, you are. Burn your inner fire brightly so that what is within will radiate without.

Journey on!

Insight #302

You are going to stir things up in your life and make some incredible changes that will place you on that "right path—to your destiny." Be ready. It is your time!

Journey on!

Insight #303

If you have ever been grounded, beached, fallen, battered, beaten, or let down, you know it is not permanent. You are focused and know that nothing will keep you from your right future.

Journey on!

Insight #304

An abundant future is awaiting you. With each step forward, you are moving to success and fulfillment. Do not stop. Do not allow yourself to give up.

Journey on!

Vivacious

Insight #305

Remember that impossible simply means you haven't found the way to make it possible yet. Your moment is soon to arrive. Let it happen.

Journey on!

Insight #306

What you allow to stay and find refuge in your mind will impact all that you do. Choose wisely, for you hold the key to open or close the door to what you allow into your inner spirit.

Journey on!

Insight #307

Do you have an attitude of forward movement or have you given up and find yourself stuck. We never stop growing, learning, or changing until the day we die, unless you have permitted yourself to already die within. Have an attitude of forward movement.

Journey on!

Insight #308

You are about to have a breakthrough and attain a new level of success and achievement in your life. Embrace it! Have it propel you even further on your path.

Journey on!

Strength

Insight #309

Be bold! You have one life to make your statement and journey to your destiny.

Journey on!

Insight #310

You are encouraged to dream. It's free, easy, and fun. However, to make your dreams come true as you travel your path, you must wake up!

Journey on!

Insight #311

By choosing to accept responsibility and the consequences that go along, you are actually choosing freedom of self.

Journey on!

Insight #312

Be bold, be a risk taker, and give your all to others. Your generosity, kindness, and caring will produce an incredible life's journey for you.

Journey on!

Exceptional

Insight #313

Your hopes and your dreams will not always be realized. But realize that hope reins eternal and dreaming is the beginning of what may become your reality.

Journey on!

Insight #314

As love grows within you, so does your beautiful spirit and your soul expands and radiates forth.

Journey on!

Insight #315

Risks must be taken in order to grow, to live, love, and experience all that life has to offer you. Without risk, we become stagnant and die.

Journey on!

Insight #316

Take your journey! Chart your course of action! Move to your destiny! It's everything you desire and it awaits for you to embrace it.

Journey on!

Delightful

Insight #317

As you travel down your life's path, you will not find your "self" but you will create it with each step you take.
Journey on!

Insight #318

Experience can be a challenging part of your journey. It is similar to taking an exam and then studying for it.
Journey on!

Insight #319

An archer will never hit his target if he is not focused on where he wants the arrow to go. Your focus of attention is critical in order to stay on your course to achieve your destiny.
Journey on!

Insight #320

When you think like a person of action, it will radiate outward and become your reality.
Journey on!

Respect

Respect

Don't expect anyone else to make you successful; it's a do-it-yourself project.

RE Hollis

Insight #321

Consider your skills, abilities, and the environment you are in and then take action with what you have to obtain that which you desire.

Journey on!

Insight #322

Count your blessings and never forget all the wonderful positive things that have happened in your life. They have brought you to where you are today!

Journey on!

Insight #323

Give all you can with all you've got and optimize every moment in your life!

Journey on!

Insight #324

You will have heartaches on your journey. They are there to test and strengthen you. Each step is taking you closer to your destiny.

Journey on!

Absorbing

Insight #325

You are ready and equal to whatever challenge you will be presented with on your Life's Journey. You are a person of power and your strength will carry you forward.
Journey on!

Insight #326

Your concern should not be who is going to let you take your journey, but who is going to stand in your way and possibly prevent you from moving forward?
Journey on!

Insight #327

Your love, affection, and at times forgiveness is needed by you as much as anybody else in your life. Do this and then move forward!
Journey on!

Insight #328

Do you energize and fuel yourself up or sap your strength, energy, and creative ability each day? You require that "fuel" to spark your strength and carry you forward.
Journey on!

Nurturing

Insight #329

The tough times you experience will allow you to grow, learn, and achieve many levels of success.
Journey on!

Insight #330

The solution is there for you. Imagine it, desire it, and enthusiastically take the appropriate actions and it will happen!
Journey on!

Insight #331

Remember that you are not looking for the path of another, but creating and following your own unique trail. That is your journey. That is your life!
Journey on!

Insight #332

Don't be intimidated by the challenges, negativity, and obstacles before you. Your inner force will propel you forward!
Journey on!

Genuine

Insight #333

With every step forward you take today you are creating what you desire to become tomorrow.

Journey on!

Insight #334

When you make the best of yourself, you are then prepared to enrich and assist others.

Journey on!

Insight #335

Your courage will allow you to step up the rungs of your ladder each day. Your vision will cause you to properly position that ladder to take you where you want to go.

Journey on!

Insight #336

If you think these thoughts or speak these words, you have already defeated yourself. "I can't...," "If only...," "I cannot go on..." These are defeating statements that should not be in your vocabulary.

Journey on!

Alert

Insight #337

The largest room you possess is "room for improvement." Never lose your thirst for knowledge, growth, and self-development.
Journey on!

Insight #338

Your time is so precious. Please do not waste it, for it is a part of your life and once lost, you can never get it back.
Journey on!

Insight #339

Persist, be determined, continually move forward, and test yourself, for that is how we discover who we are.
Journey on!

Insight #340

You are writing your life's story with each step you take. As you add each chapter, it is starting to come together and make sense. You also realize that there are more stories to tell and more chapters to write.
Journey on!

Explore

Explore

LIFE'S JOURNEY

Chart your course to your final destination

Life's Journey Pledge

This is my Life's Journey. I am the only one who can chart my course. My decisions and my actions will determine my direction and my final destination. I will find my place to stand and build the right future.

_____   _____
Signature   Date

RE Hollis

Insight #341

Each time you step forward, you are moving to the light of your future. The radiance of your vision is complemented by your purpose, while your goals and focus keep you in proper alignment.

Journey on!

Insight #342

You contain a vast treasure of knowledge, ideas, behaviors, skills, and experiences. Only you can open this fortune to have it propel you forward on your charted course.

Journey on!

Insight #343

What do you want out of your life? What do you like to do? What is your passion and true love of life? Therein lies your purpose.

Journey on!

Insight #344

Your destiny, your future, the master plan for which you have charted your course and set your sails, and that final destination is your vision.

Journey on!

Appreciate

Insight #345

When you know your purpose and have identified your vision, it is now time to set goals that will move you step-by-step toward that end. That end is in fact the "right future" you have created!

Journey on!

Insight #346

There is nothing ordinary about you. You are an extraordinary person. In fact, you are the only one capable of traveling your path and creating your future.

Journey on!

Insight #347

Negativity, putdowns, harsh comments, discouragements, and those who push you down are the links of a huge chain wrapped around you, disabling you from your destiny. You hold the key to release the chains freeing yourself to move on.

Journey on!

Insight #348

Do not discredit yourself. If you express doubt, fear, and allow intimidation to overpower you, you will become a spectator watching others on their journey. Give yourself permission to take your journey and create that future that is yours.

Journey on!

Energized

Insight #349

On your journey you will discover potential you never even realized you possess. The demands, challenges, and many opportunities your journey presents you with will allow you to boldly open the floodgates of your inner being.

Journey on!

Insight #350

You have the power! Be careful not to talk yourself out of your destiny. Rather, talk yourself into each step moving you to your future.

Journey on!

Insight #351

Don't just exist, day after day, breathing in and out. Make life happen and experience things that will take your breath away! It's your life!

Journey on!

Insight #352

You have but one life. One journey to love, to talk, to share your inner spirit and radiate outward to others. Don't delay. Embrace every moment in time.

Journey on!

Prepared

Insight #353

The spoken word once spoken cannot be taken back. Think before you speak, for your words touch the lives of others. Comment with kindness.

Journey on!

Insight #354

Don't overlook high touch in this rushed, fast-paced, quick, disposable, throwaway, and "delete" world we live in. You are the critical balance—the human factor!

Journey on!

Insight #355

As you are making a living, don't forget to make a life. As time passes with every precious moment, as you add years to your life, be certain that you add a beautiful life to your years.

Journey on!

Insight #356

Your timing is a critical element of your success and direction. Your thoughts and actions must be coordinated to promote a perfect takeoff to your intentions.

Journey on!

Promotion

Insight #357

You are ready to progress forward and one reason is your timing. You know when to recognize an opportunity and when to take action. What are you waiting for?
Journey on!

Insight #358

We all need love, warm hugs, and kisses sincerely given with kindness and caring and all from the heart and from your inner being.
Journey on!

Insight #359

There are those who listen and those who wait to start talking. Listening is an art you must master, for you will learn so much from others by being quiet, taking it all in, and learning.
Journey on!

Insight #360

Be the one who speaks up. Take advantage of the opportunities before you. Send up a rocket, make a statement, and enthusiastically take action.
Journey on!

Cheerful

1,000 Ways in 1,000 Days to Win from Within!

Cheerful

Don't be discouraged, it's usually the last key in the bunch that opens the door.

RE Hollis

Insight #361

The lucky are those who take advantage of the opportunities this beautiful journey presents and the unlucky are those who don't. You will give yourself permission to not only recognize but communicate and act on those opportunities for they will stretch and lead you to new horizons.

Journey on!

Insight #362

Some days there are moments when you feel like what's the use of continuing on? That is when your inner being will propel you forward with the strength to carry on.

Journey on!

Insight #363

Do not derail the fundamental transformation from where you are to where you need to be. That is the essence of your journey. That is your destiny!

Journey on!

Insight #364

It's easy to focus on the "outer space" around you. However, your inner space is critical for you to feed and nurture, for that is what will radiate out to touch others.

Journey on!

Noble

Insight #365

When you arrive, you will know for it is the total package of every single step that you have taken and every page you have written in your own book of life.

Journey on!

Insight #366

What mentality do you have? Is your mentality one that limits you, points out what you are lacking and promotes an "I can't do that" attitude or does it speak abundance, success, and victory? It's your choice!

Journey on!

Insight #367

Quit, fail, give up—these are not words in your vocabulary. You will not even consider any possibility of defeat. Persistence, determination, victory, and success are yours! Take it!

Journey on!

Insight #368

You are constantly creating your "right future." Each step, every day, is moving you nearer to your destiny.

Journey on!

Justice

Insight #369

What are you certain about? There rests your purpose, confidence, values, and beliefs. That certainty will overcome your doubt, fear, and struggles.
Journey on!

Insight #370

A true "master" is never satisfied and never becomes too comfortable. In order to have an overflow of success, you must be open to continuous growth, knowledge, and skills.
Journey on!

Insight #371

There is usually "no quick fix." Your time, endurance, determination, and stick-to-it-tiveness will get you there. So many give up when on the brink of success. Not you! Hold on, it's coming!
Journey on!

Insight #372

When you shed all those fears, doubts, frustrations, and distractions that hold you back, you will then develop an abundant mentality that will drive you forward!
Journey on!

Crossroads

Insight #373

Each morning, set your course of confidence, determination, and focus. Every evening, reflect and be grateful for what you have accomplished and the distance covered that day. Then prepare for tomorrow. Your next step!

Journey on!

Insight #374

There will be those who only speak a poor and defeated language to you. They put you down, attempt to remove your confidence, determination, enthusiasm, and success mentality. Move away and distance yourself from these individuals. They will extinguish your fire if you allow it. Run to your light!

Journey on!

Insight #375

As you are traveling your path, don't become stuck at a place that is not your future. Where you are is not where you are going. Abundance will be yours when you decide to move forward.

Journey on!

Insight #376

You do deserve it! Abundance and success are yours if you can shake off the obstacles that are before you, holding you down, and step up to your destiny!

Journey on!

Truth

Insight #377

Write your "Life's Story." Make it an epic adventure. There are many chapters of renewal, hope, and victory. Only you can author your story.

Journey on!

Insight #378

Get ready! Your future is about to reveal itself and make amazing changes that will take you to that next level.

Journey on!

Insight #379

A new season is in your future. Things are going to begin to blossom for you. New opportunities will be recognized and capitalized upon.

Journey on!

Insight #380

Let go of the past. It holds you down and keeps you from moving forward. You cannot live in it or grow. Look to your future. Embrace it. There lie the changes that will move you to your destiny.

Journey on!

Master

Master

Get out of your comfort zone and soar to new heights.

RE Hollis

Insight #381

You can't just see what lies ahead. You must have vision, direction, purpose, goals, and a desire to take action and responsibility.

Journey on!

Insight #382

This is a year of positive change. Your time of waiting, wishing, and hoping is over. Your actions are going to make the difference.

Journey on!

Insight #383

Impossible just means you haven't found the solution yet. Keep moving forward.

Journey on!

Insight #384

Don't be a skeptic or a doubter. Your future will reveal itself to you, all in good time. Each action, each movement forward takes you closer to your destiny!

Journey on!

Zest

Insight #385

Where are you right at this moment in your life with your relationships, job, education, health, psychological well-being, etc. That is the starting point from which you will build your future.

Journey on!

Insight #386

You must be able to completely trust yourself. When you do, it is so powerful. Work hard not to shatter that trust, for it becomes one of your driving forces.

Journey on!

Insight #387

You must fulfill your destiny and travel your path on your own. Many will influence and guide you, but the final decision and choice is yours.

Journey on!

Insight #388

Sometimes there is no logical explanation to the events that unfold in your life. Know that each piece of the puzzle plays a significant role in forming the final picture. You will achieve clarity of understanding.

Journey on!

Viable

Insight #389

Love is the answer. Love of life and all you carry in your heart will now radiate outward. You are going to blossom forth, experience favor, and have a bounding leap forward, reaching new levels of achievement.

Journey on!

Insight #390

Enjoy every moment of your journey. You never know exactly which particular turn in the road will have a magnificent impact on your life.

Journey on!

Insight #391

Don't dismiss the little things in your life. Greatness can come of them. One small item may just be that which turns into something extraordinary, impacting your life in ways you've never imagined.

Journey on!

Insight #392

Think big, be bold, look with vision, and you will go further than you ever imagine. You can push yourself beyond your understanding and beyond what you believe are your limitations.

Journey on!

Aptitude

Insight #393

Make a difference with your life. Strive for a new, higher level of achievement. Don't settle for less when your destiny is more that will move you forward.
Journey on!

Insight #394

Don't be quick to dismiss those things that are brought to your attention. They may hold the key to move you to a higher level where the vision is something to behold!
Journey on!

Insight #395

Be radical. Take off the limitations you have set for yourself and allow yourself to stretch your very boundaries. What an exciting journey lies before you!
Journey on!

Insight #396

Extraordinary people are just ordinary people who have given themselves permission to do extraordinary things. Do not settle for mediocrity. Live, be, and achieve your destiny.
Journey on!

Stunning

Insight #397

Day after day, each week, month, and year you are fulfilling your purpose by aligning your actions with your goals, mission, and vision. Every moment counts!

Journey on!

Insight #398

Do not sell yourself short. You are capable of amazing things. The path you go down is your choice. Take the high road to the next level.

Journey on!

Insight #399

Don't set limitations on yourself, for there are no limitations except for those you create. Now get busy and do it!

Journey on!

Insight #400

Make one more effort on your part to move forward, one more positive thought about where you are going, and one more moment of focusing all that is in your heart. It will make a difference!

Journey on!

Special

Special

Don't go so fast on your
Life's Journey that you miss
the sign for new opportunities.

RE Hollis

Awareness Promotes Effectiveness

Choose Amazing and Stay Your Course!

Choose amazing and stay your course!

Feeling lost? Embrace your Purpose! Uncertain as to where you are going? Review your Goals! Ready to give in, give up, quit? Stay the course!

It is your Vision, your directional beacon, your future! Doubt and uncertainty on a regular basis may be indicators that you are not being true to self. Listen to that inner spirit. Allow that inner being to be your guide and radiate outward. Let it guide you to your "right future."

When you understand your purpose and vision for your life the goals, you set each day become so much easier. If they move you forward and reflect your purpose, do it! If they take you away from that master plan and charted course, don't do it! Easy to grasp but challenging to implement.

Your direction, your plan, your map is right there before you—follow it. It will take you to your future! Be amazing! Why would you choose anything else?

Insight #401

You are not a perfect being. You are a human being. You will make mistakes. At times, you will fail. Forgive yourself and get over it. Continue to move forward!
Journey on!

Insight #402

You may not understand exactly why something is happening, but know that each step is moving you forward to your destiny.
Journey on!

Insight #403

If you stay true to your purpose, mission, vision, and goals, you will continue to move in the direction of your future. Through difficulties, storms, challenges, and trying times, your compass will continually bring you back to the right path.
Journey on!

Insight #404

Don't stay focused on a current discouragement. It is a moment in the time of your life and not meant to hold permanent residence. Learn and move on.
Journey on!

Esteem

Insight #405

Opportunities will present themselves every step of the way on your journey. Be prepared to recognize and take action when called upon.

Journey on!

Insight #406

You have a purpose, a destiny to fulfill. Let nothing stop you from taking each step in the direction of your future. Embrace each moment with the understanding that you are moving to a higher level.

Journey on!

Insight #407

Stop and take a moment to remember why you are on this remarkable journey. That is your purpose and the real reason you are on this venture of life.

Journey on!

Insight #408

Listen to your body and to your inner voice. It lets you know when it is time to re-energize, rest, sharpen your saw to avoid catastrophes, and carry on.

Journey on!

Intimacy

Insight #409

Your destiny awaits you and is all part of a master plan. It is not always a straight line but filled with turns and curves that reflect our humanity. Stay firm, for the path will lead you to your future.

Journey on!

Insight #410

Don't ever get so immersed in life that you fail to hear that inner voice to guide you on your journey. It reflects your inner being.

Journey on!

Insight #411

Be gentle with yourself. You have much to do and a long journey to take. Treat yourself with kindness as you prepare for what lies ahead.

Journey on!

Insight #412

When you are all alone, remember that you still have yourself, and that is extraordinary!

Journey on!

Clarity

Insight #413

Take a moment and celebrate what you have accomplished thus far. Now get yourself ready for the next goal you have before you and do it!

Journey on!

Insight #414

As you travel on your life's journey, you will thrive more from what you give to others rather than what you keep. Yet, you will receive an abundance!

Journey on!

Insight #415

Don't dwell on what might have been, but focus on making it happen. For the moment you give into doubt, you will no longer allow access to that portion of your journey.

Journey on!

Insight #416

Stop making excuses and start making results. Take the actions that will move you in the direction of your destiny.

Journey on!

Well-being

Insight #417

A difficult change in your life can be a good occurrence, for it may be the one item that repositions you to turn a corner placing your closer to your destiny, your future.
Journey on!

Insight #418

Your inner attitude and spirit will bedazzle your outer self. Let it radiate out and light your way!
Journey on!

Insight #419

Difficulties, challenging situations, and frustrations are to be expected, for they are all a part of the process that is shaping, fine tuning, and sharpening your skills.
Journey on!

Insight #420

Participation in life is such a glorious thing, yet so many choose to sit on the sidelines and watch. You will not do that! Take life by the horns and ride it for all that it has to offer.
Journey on!

Wow

Wow

Did you ever wonder why some birds stay in the same place when they can fly anywhere?

Did you ever ask yourself the same question since you are free to do the same?

Insight #421

As long as you stay focused on other people's events, going down other people's paths and their journey prevents you from having an event of your own or a personal path to follow. Make your own statement in life!
Journey on!

Insight #422

I will never be the same. With each step forward I take, I am changing, transitioning, and rearranging my life to stay in sync with my directional beacon—my future!
Journey on!

Insight #423

We each have good and negative characteristics as part of our humanity. It's up to you to encourage, strengthen, and activate the positive ones that will raise you up to a higher level.
Journey on!

Insight #424

You do not have to accept discouragement; you can control it. You can choose to carry on to a better, more prosperous and abundant you.
Journey on!

Warmth

Insight #425

Shake off the negative, defeating thoughts. Control the path you are taking. Start right now, this very moment in time. It's your choice and you hold the key!
Journey on!

Insight #426

This is your time. This is your moment. However, you must make the choice to energize the moment and make it happen! You are the critical element in the equation.
Journey on!

Insight #427

If you live in and embrace the past, it can bring you to a grinding halt. You do not have to be held as a prisoner by negative things that have already happened. You will shake that off and move forward.
Journey on!

Insight #428

You can overcome whatever you choose to overcome. Your choices set your course. Choose honor, trust, respect, love, integrity, and make it happen!
Journey on!

Liberal

Insight #429

Don't circumvent the correct path you should be on. Grasp your focus, purpose, and vision. They will provide the directional beacon to keep you on the right course.

Journey on!

Insight #430

It is up to you. You will never change what you tolerate. So often waiting for others or something to change can be frustrating. The one thing you can control is you. You must be the change.

Journey on!

Insight #431

You will find that staying on course to achieve your destiny will make you happy, confident, fulfilled, and charged with a desire to achieve even more.

Journey on!

Insight #432

You will find that getting off course in the achievement of your destiny will leave you confused, upset, frustrated, and deflated. You will lose your desire to carry on. Fuel your fire with positive, uplifting, and high level items that keep you focused and on course.

Journey on!

Curious

Insight #433

You need to deal with not "what was" nor what you are "wishing and hoping for," but to face the reality of your "real" world. That is the true starting point you will build your future upon.

Journey on!

Insight #434

Are you happy, fulfilled, and anxious to get up each day and be surrounded by others who lift you up and encourage your actions? Then you are focused and living with purpose, vision, and goals that are "right!"

Journey on!

Insight #435

Will it benefit you, move you forward, and assist in fulfilling your destiny? If the answer is "No," then why are you doing it or even paying attention to it? If "Yes," move forward with confidence!

Journey on!

Insight #436

Have you ever been willing to fight and lose everything for what you believe in? Don't lose—be amazing!

Journey on!

Alive

Insight #437

Do you know the power of your own voice? You have the capability to speak the truth! The truth will out!

Journey on!

Insight #438

Whether you are well established or just starting on your journey you will discover something remarkable. It is your journey and you will go farther even if you cannot see, but you possess a vision.

Journey on!

Insight #439

Are you just trying to understand your place in the world or to fight for it? Believe in the strength, ability, and power you possess and achieve your destiny.

Journey on!

Insight #440

You are not just another number in this world. You are an extraordinary individual who is moving ever forward on your path.

Journey on!

Harmony

Harmony

You can't change the people around you, but you are free to change the people you are around!

Insight #441

You will find the strength to confront any foe, conquer any challenge, and carry on!

Journey on!

Insight #442

You will cross common ground with others. The value of the beliefs you share are stronger than what divides you.

Journey on!

Insight #443

Your path, your journey is your home. Cherish it, protect it, nurture it, and travel that road confidently for it will lead you to your future.

Journey on!

Insight #444

Pay it forward! You are the result of so many people and experiences. Share your genius with others and assist them on their journey.

Journey on!

Terrific

Insight #445

Have the biggest and boldest dreams that you can imagine. Reach out with a beacon of belief in the impossible and make it possible.

Journey on!

Insight #446

The actions you take and the decisions you make on a daily basis will move you forward while creating incredible change.

Journey on!

Insight #447

You will have to make difficult choices, and you will disappoint some people. Do not disappoint yourself.

Journey on!

Insight #448

Cross those lines of difference. Your walk, your journey is to take the path to your destiny. Keep going forward as each step moves you closer. Don't give up! Do not quit. Achieve and be amazing!

Journey on!

Dignity

Insight #449

What burden weighs you down? You will have worries and challenges before you. Stay the course! Each movement forward will refresh you!

Journey on!

Insight #450

What are those key issues you deal with in your life? Awareness promotes effectiveness! Sacrifices must be made, but be certain to focus your energies properly.

Journey on!

Insight #451

What will lessen your troubles and all that makes you weary? Each step you take will provide the solution as it moves you closer to your destiny.

Journey on!

Insight #452

Yes! There will be times when you feel like throwing in the proverbial towel, quitting and giving up all your dreams, your destiny, your future. You will not do that. You will persevere and carry on!

Journey on!

Discipline

Insight #453

Do you want to see yourself in an EPIC novel? Write your unique story. You are the only one who can author and live that work!

Journey on!

Insight #454

When your inner spirit is determined to give you advice, listen well, for it will be delivered whether you choose to be receptive or not.

Journey on!

Insight #455

What does this day hold for you? Each morning take a moment to allow the day to come into alignment with your purpose, vision, and goals. You will be focused!

Journey on!

Insight #456

You cannot even imagine the benefits you will receive for all you give to others, the service you provide, and the gifts you share. Ah, it's a secret of the YOUniverse and a requirement for a purposeful journey.

Journey on!

Beneficial

Insight #457

Allow your inner being to teach you what you are ready to learn. Do not ignore that spirit for it will guide you to your destiny!

Journey on!

Insight #458

Messages and advice you receive from guides along your journey are cordial to your inner being. Receive them with gratitude and humility.

Journey on!

Insight #459

Don't leave behind any strangers on your path. Before you continue on your journey, they are to become your friend.

Journey on!

Insight #460

Be certain to take moments to be silly, foolish, and light-hearted. It cleanses and refreshes the spirit while renewing your strength.

Journey on!

Obsession

Obsession

Life has no remote;
get up and change it yourself.

RE Hollis

Insight #461

Take time to rest, sharpen your skills, review your goals, and align yourself with the charted course of your Life's Map.
Journey on!

Insight #462

You have been given an opportunity to travel to your destiny. What a remarkable journey lies before you. With each step you take, move forward with expectations of an abundant future.
Journey on!

Insight #463

You need to do it! Stand up, take charge, and move forward. You are right where you need to be, but to move to where you are going, it's up to you.
Journey on!

Insight #464

Listen, listen, listen to the "real" world around you. Then "realize" where your "real" lies and move in that direction.
Journey on!

Colossal

Insight #465

Develop your ability to concentrate, focus, and pay attention to the directions coming from your inner being. That guidance will show you the way to your destiny.
Journey on!

Insight #466

Do you desire to have an "easier" life? Why do you ignore your inner voice? Your inner spirit will guide and direct you.
Journey on!

Insight #467

Your path of escape is the road to your future. There are the answers and solutions you have been looking for. Behold, it is right there before you.
Journey on!

Insight #468

Decisions must be made with each step forward you take. Your "Big Picture"—the purpose, mission, vision, and goals of your life together—chart the path of your Life's Journey. When your actions are in alignment, you will confidently move forward.
Journey on!

Focus

Insight #469

Who is leading, guiding, advising, and directing you to your future? Are you properly tuned in? Listen with clarity and make the choices of your life.

Journey on!

Insight #470

Do not ignore the inner spirit that is guiding you. Those prompts cause you to think, focus, and stay the course of your life.

Journey on!

Insight #471

As you travel through life, look, be, and do your very best each day. Be amazing! You are creating your own right future through your daily actions.

Journey on!

Insight #472

Are you a getter or a giver? The real rewards and personal growth will come from what you give.

Journey on!

Promotion

Insight #473

Are you in touch will the "real you?" It is worth taking the time for you are the best you there will ever be. Why not be amazing!
Journey on!

Insight #474

You have all the time there will ever be. You cannot make more time. Your time is precious and there is no opportunity for a do over. Be focused and live your purpose.
Journey on!

Insight #475

You have been given a gift. It is called today. Keep it in alignment with the course you have charted for your life. Your purpose, vision, and goals, should direct you and be acted upon at each precious moment.
Journey on!

Insight #476

Are you being your best you? When you are focused on your true direction, your purposeful journey, then your concentration and confidence will be true to your real self. Be amazing!
Journey on!

Brilliance

Insight #477

Each evening, count your blessings for all you have accomplished and the steps you have taken toward your destiny. Each morning, refocus, get back on track, and on course to your future.

Journey on!

Insight #478

Do not tolerate those who complain, are negative, unmotivated, and have no sense of direction. They will hold you back, bring you down, and keep you from your right future.

Journey on!

Insight #479

Appreciate all the individuals who have helped and assisted you on a portion of your journey. However, realize when it is time to move on and attain each next level. Choose wisely for it will lift you up or take you down. Be amazing!

Journey on!

Insight #480

Do they understand your destiny? If not, then why do you continue to associate with them? You need to distance yourself from those who do not support, believe, lift, push, encourage, and inspire you. When you surround yourself with the right people, you will be amazing!

Journey on!

Success

Success

If you don't like where you are, then change it! You're not a tree.

RE Hollis

Insight #481

When someone takes you off your chosen course, your purposeful journey, you cannot blame them. It is your choice, your responsibility to stay the course that will take you to your right future.

Journey on!

Insight #482

Work to enhance the inner attitude of your very being and you will change the outer aspects of life as that attitude radiates outward to others.

Journey on!

Insight #483

Get out and live your life. Your dreams will not become significant realities if you do not permit your inner world and spirit to come out.

Journey on!

Insight #484

Give yourself permission to dare and risk, for that will allow you to deal with the difficulties of life.

Journey on!

Extraordinary

Insight #485

Demonstrate understanding and gentleness with all that you encounter on your path. It makes each step of your journey worthwhile.

Journey on!

Insight #486

The Japanese have an expression, "Too many minds." Essentially it refers to "too many distractions" preventing you from having a precise focus of attention to accomplish your goal. Do not have "too many minds." Focus, Focus, Focus!

Journey on!

Insight #487

If you do not take care of your own self, you will not be able to care for others. Strengthen your core, your inner being, and then you will radiate out to others.

Journey on!

Insight #488

Someone needs your kindness, your belief, your confidence. It may be the one item an individual needs to turn down that right path to their own destiny. Be amazing, be extraordinary and do not miss the opportunity to reach out to others. When you help others, your own life will be abundant!

Journey on!

Responsiveness

Insight #489

The tasks before you become so much easier when we begin to take action. The real thief of your time and energy is procrastination.

Journey on!

Insight #490

Difficulties and trouble are an inevitable part of life. They will come, but you will have your head held high knowing that you will defeat them.

Journey on!

Insight #491

Take those who have used their comforting skills with you by the hand and embrace them. They have given and shared with you from their heart.

Journey on!

Insight #492

When you know an action needs to be taken, why wait? Set your "amazing" into action and be the necessary change! Give yourself permission to do that which you know is right. Do it!

Journey on!

Expressiveness

Insight #493

Periodically stop, pause, and reflect on where you are at and where you need to be. Then continue to move forward on your path to your destiny.

Journey on!

Insight #494

Don't forget to participate in life. Your observations, analyses, and judgments have their place, but life is not meant to be a spectator sport.

Journey on!

Insight #495

The opportunities for growth are limitless. Have a balance between your focus on others and self and move beyond your expectations.

Journey on!

Insight #496

There is no ceiling, no summit, no limitations to the success you will achieve except for the boundaries you place upon yourself.

Journey on!

Summit

Insight #497

Are you listening? Are you tuned in to your inner being and allowing it to guide, prompt, and counsel your actions? Trust your inner sprit.

Journey on!

Insight #498

No one can change your attitude or your inner peace without your permission. You are the guard of the bridge to your soul. What and who are you allowing in?

Journey on!

Insight #499

You cannot control the actions of others and often cannot change them. However, you can control "YOU" and make the decision to control what you allow in that will fuel you spirit, lift you up, and move you forward.

Journey on!

Insight #500

Your YOUniverse awaits you. Create the future you desire by taking the appropriate actions every day that will catapult you to achieving your destiny!

Journey on!

Catapult

Catapult

Only you have the power to manage your own Life's Journey.

Awareness Promotes Effectiveness

Give More Than You Take! Embrace the Right People!

Don't ever get so "big for your boots" that your ego takes over and you forget all that happened to get you to where you are. Please and thank you still go a long way. Always remember the "Golden Rule." If you want to not only remain where you are but continuously achieve even higher levels, remain humble and grateful for all you have. Count your blessings each day. Surround yourself with people you know, like, trust, admire and respect. Give more than you take!

Embrace the right people and welcome them into your life. Those who bring the gifts of excellence, inspiration, kindness, integrity, passion, consideration, success, love, and who know where they are going. They will lift you up, celebrate you, sharpen your skills and knowledge, and assist and prepare you for the rest of your life's journey. We have gathered the right people together to provide guidance, encouragement, and a sharing of performance-based actions that will keep you on course, provide a directional beacon to your right future. They represent your total package of wholeness.

Many individuals allow themselves to be:
- Mediocre
- Hot tempered
- Disrespectful
- Small minded
- Poisonous
- Stuck
- Negative
- Bring you down
- Hold on, keep you where you are at

Distance yourself from those who divert you from your chosen path. Just like the booster rockets that assisted with lift off, there comes a time when separation is necessary. They have served a purpose and cannot take you any farther.

The qualities of your friends will influence your qualities. Be careful who you spend your time with and set boundaries for yourself. You have the ability to make choices.

Associate with dreamers, Eagles, and companions who will make you soar!

Are you protecting all your beliefs, all that you stand for, and desire?

Everyone is not following your path. You will find that as you achieve higher levels, your group becomes smaller, more unique, connected, and focused.

There are times in your life when you cannot do the carrying but will lighten your load and assist you on your journey.

Cultivate relationships that will inspire and lift you up.

You need the right people to build your support team of success.

You still have a long way to go on your journey and the best is yet to come. More to discover, people to meet, new levels to be attained.

Magic moments will happen to you. Be ready to follow your calling, your purpose. It will come over you, be fearless. It is your life. Advance in the direction of your dream, your heart, your imagination.

Insight #501

Achieve a new level of success by allowing your inner spirit to radiate outward. Then you will find victory, abundance, and move beyond your expectations as a result of the action you have chosen to take.

Journey on!

Insight #502

Stop complaining and being negative. You will start moving forward when you start making things happen and not waiting on others to do it for you.

Journey on!

Insight #503

The right place, at the right time, for the right reasons, with the right people does not just happen. You have been years in planning and preparation for what appears to have suddenly taken place. Your "overnight success" may have taken years!

Journey on!

Insight #504

Refresh yourself, sharpen your skills, fine tune and review your goals. Then continue on your journey. You will make it to that "right future" you are creating.

Journey on!

Refresh

Insight #505

Keep doing the right things and be patient. You will arrive at where you need to be. When you live from within, your talents, skills, and abilities will come together to achieve that next level.

Journey on!

Insight #506

Deal with people you know, like, trust, admire, and respect. They will feed and nurture your inner spirit and move you in the direction of your destiny.

Journey on!

Insight #507

Those you are able to be vulnerable with are incredibly important people in your life. With them you are real! You lay all your cards on the table and can be completely open. That's a level of trust few reach.

Journey on!

Insight #508

Your declaration of faith and values—the pledge—will cause you to overcome all that lies in your path. That is where your strength, determination, and courage lies to accomplish your destiny.

Journey on!

Declaration

Insight #509

That's right! Step forward! It sounds simple to grasp the concept that we must move in that chosen direction. However, the challenge is implementation for only you can give yourself the permission to take action. Be amazing! Do it!
Journey on!

Insight #510

Make your opportunities happen. Be the catalyst. Don't wait for that special moment to take place. Create it and be the necessary change. Watch for the abundant results of your actions.
Journey on!

Insight #511

So you got a bad deal in life. You don't care for the cards you have been dealt. Get over it and get on with it! You hold the necessary change within you. Release that energy and take action!
Journey on!

Insight #512

The power of your words can move you from ordinary to extraordinary. It gives life and brings your purpose, vision, goals, dreams, ideas, and desires into reality.
Journey on!

Grasp

Insight #513

Be amazing! Think it, proclaim it, and act on it. Do it! Have a magnificent obsession with each step you take and embrace your destiny.

Journey on!

Insight #514

Take the time to have real interactions with others on your journey. High tech items and devices are marvelous tools from the mind of man, but they should not replace or overpower high touch—the human factor!

Journey on!

Insight #515

Pursue opportunity with each step forward you take. Be on guard, ever vigilant, prepared to take action, and move forward.

Journey on!

Insight #516

Don't ignore goals because when you finish one, another awaits you. That is your very life blood. Welcome each new goal with excitement and enthusiasm. Your inner spirit will radiate outward!

Journey on!

Proclaim

Insight #517

Your life is like an incredible epic book. Be aware of the page you are currently on and what you are writing. It's your story. Be amazing!

Journey on!

Insight #518

Every day review, reflect, and declare the amazing items you will embrace with abundance that will move you forward. You are amazing!

Journey on!

Insight #519

When you are in awe of things happening around you, take the time to look out the window of your life and take it all in. Appreciate the glorious journey you are on!

Journey on!

Insight #520

Remember those who have come before you and assisted in paving portions of your journey. They have each had an impact on the devious you make and the direction you move in.

Journey on!

Devious

Devious

I prefer running
   in the morning...
before my brain figures out
   what I'm doing!

RE Hollis

Insight #521

Do not let fears of making a mistake or failing stop you in your tracks. You are a human being, not a perfect being; you will make mistakes. It's how you react and respond to them that really matters. Learn and stay the course to your future.

Journey on!

Insight #522

You must continue your journey. It is taking you to your future and each step taken will move you closer to your destiny.

Journey on!

Insight #523

Those who do not promote you are not needed in your life. If they do not lift you up, encourage, and believe in you, think of it as their way of saying goodbye. Release them and experience a new freedom that will catapult you to your destiny.

Journey on!

Insight #524

You may wander on your path for what seems an unending period of time. You may even at times feel lost and confused—stay your course! It will all come together. Each step is moving you closer to your right future.

Journey on!

Freedom

Insight #525

In order for you to be successful on your journey, you need to have a "sense of urgency." Focus on and pay attention to those items and people who will assist with the appropriate knowledge and skills to take you to the next level.
Journey on!

Insight #526

Are you focusing on your business and purpose? Attending meetings and events that do not relate to your "direction for success" are usually a waste of your time. If you merely want to socialize, then make that your purpose and forget the other. It's your choice! Put in the proper amount of time, effort, and energy where it will benefit and support your cause!
Journey on!

Insight #527

As you journey on, remember that you have a plan, a purpose, and a vision that provides you with a directional beacon lighting your way to your destiny. You will come through the storm to sunny days and a brightness you never even anticipated.
Journey on!

Insight #528

Life is not perfect; we are not perfect beings but human beings. We will err, we will fail, we will experience defeat, and difficulties. Don't be consumed by those gathering clouds but stay your course and realize that you will persevere.
Journey on!

Benefit

Insight #529

Your future is filled with abundance. You have this before you but the door must be opened. The key must be turned. You hold the means to accomplishing this. Be amazing. Take the actions to create it!

Journey on!

Insight #530

Your future is there for the taking. With each step you are moving to your destiny. It is yours to achieve. It is awaiting your action. Only you can do it!

Journey on!

Insight #531

Do you radiate your inner spirit outward to reflect your confidence and energy or do your nonverbals send a different message? You are an amazing, prosperous, abundantly skilled individual. Unleash your spirit from within and lift those gifts to the surface for all to experience.

Journey on!

Insight #532

Your time and call to action has come. Right now, this day, this moment be amazing! What are you waiting for? The time is now, the place is here and the person is You!

Journey on!

Amazing

Insight #533

All things will pass. The obstacles, hardships, and challenges will only keep you from your destiny if you allow them. If you say, "that's it!," then "that is it!" You will be stuck. However, with your permission, the next level of achievement awaits you.

Journey on!

Insight #534

The only permanence that you should accept is abundance, success, blessings, and tears of joy! Stay your course and carry on!

Journey on!

Insight #535

There are so many people who are profoundly lonely. You do not have to be one of them. Reach out, talk, share, and be amazing!

Journey on!

Insight #536

Don't lose sight of your truth. It is your spark that lights the directional beacon to your future!

Journey on!

Permanence

Insight #537

You need some alone time each day to reflect, to count your blessings, and show gratitude for all the good you encountered that day. It strengthens your inner being and prepares you for your next step.

Journey on!

Insight #538

You have only scratched the surface of your life. There is so much more. Delve down deep into the depths of your heart, your soul, and your inner being. Make room for newness. It's coming!

Journey on!

Insight #539

Self-accountability is a powerful thing once you accept it. When you own your actions, then you have a force to create that will drive you forward.

Journey on!

Insight #540

Work, rest, play, dance, and have balance in your life. Each one nurtures and strengthens the others. You haven't seen anything yet!

Journey on!

Delve

Delve

Keep searching for the niche that is the "best fit" for you.

RE Hollis

Insight #541

You are designed, streamlined, equipped, and prepared for greatness. Use your gifts, talents, skills, and knowledge as the oars to move your vessel forward to your future.

Journey on!

Insight #542

It is time to stop thinking ordinary and start thinking extraordinary. Be amazing! Allow yourself to stretch beyond the limits of your imagination.

Journey on!

Insight #543

A true master never gets too comfortable and is never satisfied. You never stop learning as you take each next step along your journey.

Journey on!

Insight #544

A simple word or deed can have a dramatic impact upon those you meet along your path. Your respect, kindness, and caring will deliver a powerful message to others.

Journey on!

Streamlined

Insight #545

Only you can talk yourself out of your amazing! Live it, reach for it, and do it!

Journey on!

Insight #546

No matter where you are at, it is not where you are going. Be prepared to be catapulted and thrust yourself with a spirited bounding leap into your future.

Journey on!

Insight #547

It can be so difficult to move forward if the past continues to have a grip and a grasp on you. Let go and move on to your future.

Journey on!

Insight #548

Do not allow others to bring you down or contaminate your inner being. Program your mind, what you dwell upon, and where your focus is at. That will produce confidence in your ability to step into your destiny.

Journey on!

Program

Insight #549

You require a consistent focus on where you are going—not up and positive one day, down and questioning your direction the next. Identify and embrace your true purpose, vision and goals. That will allow you to stay your course.

Journey on!

Insight #550

When you fail, fail forward. When you fall, fall up! Take a moment to evaluate, grieve, and learn from it. Then be done with it and move on!

Journey on!

Insight #551

Your passion, your drive, and your destiny are all within you. You are equipped with all the tools for your own rescue.

Journey on!

Insight #552

As you travel that true path to your future, you will experience growth, abundance, opportunities, new relationships, joy, and blessings. It will all happen for you! Be amazing!

Journey on!

Identify

Insight #553

The gentle softness of the people you touch will come forth as a result of all you give and radiate outward to them. Your inner being will reflect your true self.

Journey on!

Insight #550

Cherish every friendship you have been blessed to nurture and develop. They will strengthen and lift you up to higher levels than you have ever imagined.

Journey on!

Insight #551

Dare to declare and embrace your pledge to Self! Each month we include the pledge in Life's Journey Magazine to renew your focus and commitment to self. It's your choice to stay on track and keep moving forward.

Journey on!

Insight #552

With a good wind and a good compass you can sail to the port of your choice. It's up to you, however, to set your sails and chart your course.

Journey on!

Gentleness

Insight #557

Your real freedom lies within you—your ability to make responsible choices that you hold yourself accountable for and accept the consequences of the actions you take. Once you achieve that you will set yourself free and realize the power before you.

Journey on!

Insight #558

Doing your absolute best in your "right now" moment will position you perfectly to be prepared for the next moment to follow. Each and every step forward you take is a building block to your future.

Journey on!

Insight #559

Your future will be one of gratefulness and gratitude for the positive decisions and choices you are making right now. Stay true to your course.

Journey on!

Insight #560

Look to your future. That is where you are going. Every action should be moving you in that positive direction. At the end of each day take note. How have your actions moved you forward? What made a difference?

Journey on!

Gratefulness

1,000 Ways in 1,000 Days to Win from Within!

Gratefulness

Celebrate what you've accomplished on your Life's Journey.

```
DANCE
DREAM
EXPLORE
LEARN
BE BOLD
CREATE
INNOVATE
GRATITUDE
INSPIRE
LOVE
ENJOY
```

RE Hollis

Insight #561

Don't be afraid of exposing your true self. You are an amazing individual and you need to allow your inner spirit to come forth and be shared with others.
Journey on!

Insight #562

Friendship is not to be taken lightly for you are tremendously influenced by those you surround yourself with and in turn you influence them. It is both an honor and a responsibility.
Journey on!

Insight #563

Aging is a privilege and requires strength and endurance. Every step you have taken along your path is an honor and you have acquired knowledge and skills taking you to an abundant future. Aging is the accumulative adventures of your life.
Journey on!

Insight #564

Don't let your past poison your future. Are you bitter, frustrated, angry, feeling sorry for yourself? It will take effort, but you must let it go in order to go forward. You can be discouraged and down for the rest of your life and if you allow it, you are preventing yourself from your destiny.
Journey on!

Influence

Insight #565

Have an attitude of gratitude throughout your journey. It will stay with you so much longer than just being thankful. It will touch your inner being.

Journey on!

Insight #566

Hoist up your sails and flee away from the sea of despair, discouragement, and negativism. Sail to calm waters and a safe port to lift your spirits.

Journey on!

Insight #567

Each step you take in the direction of your future is taking you away from your obstacles, frustrations, and struggles. You are moving to wholeness, joy, and success.

Journey on!

Insight #568

Respect your time to sharpen your skills, sleep, re-energize, review your master plan and course of action. These moments are sacred for they are the directional beacons of light to your future.

Journey on!

Beacons

Insight #569

Before anything, listen! How can you possibly even begin to offer solutions for yourself or others if you haven't listened? There you will find answers to move forward.

Journey on!

Insight #570

Bon voyage! Each step forward is a journey to be taken. You need to take the trip. Don't stay where you are at for it is not your final destination.

Journey on!

Insight #571

The past is past. It is over and done. The future is bright, alive, and glowing. It needs you. Your future begins today! Look forward, move forward, step forward.

Journey on!

Insight #572

There is no excuse for rudeness. Treat others the way that you would like to be treated and beyond!

Journey on!

Listen

Insight #573

Every morning charge forward! Exude a confidence belief and an attitude of gratitude and success. You are already charting your course to a bright future.

Journey on!

Insight #574

When you follow your inner spirit, you will experience a feeling of peace with self. Your inner being is guiding you to what is right to enhance your character, charisma, charm, confidence, and peace.

Journey on!

Insight #575

A moment of mourning, frustration, or sadness is normal, but to cling to that and live it your entire life is not. The rest of your life awaits you—won't you make the journey? There are so many beautiful things that lie ahead.

Journey on!

Insight #576

Be grateful for the decisions you have made each day and the service you have provided to others. Then you are well on your way to fulfillment!

Journey on!

Peace

Insight #577

Don't judge people for where they are today for it is not where they are going. They are on their journey just as you are on yours. Appreciate, understand, and respect what they are experiencing.

Journey on!

Insight #578

You should enjoy, cherish, and rejoice in the differences of each person you meet along your journey.

Journey on!

Insight #579

You don't need to be sick in order to get better. Constant improvement, growth, and understanding will take place throughout your entire journey. You never stop learning throughout the journey called "life."

Journey on!

Insight #580

You do not have to tell people they are doing something wrong; they usually already know that. Provide the guidance, encouragement, love, respect, and caring needed for those you are traveling with on each portion of your journey.

Journey on!

Rejoice

Rejoice

My manager reminded me that it is my responsibility to manage my work/play balance, so I'm thinking of replacing my laptop with a case of beer.

Insight #581

We all get dealt various degrees of suffering. When you realize that it is a part of life and it serves a purpose in shaping our destiny, it becomes more embraceable.
Journey on!

Insight #582

Find the common ground. All roads intersect somewhere along your journey. It is all part of a master plan and every twist and winding turn serves a purpose in contributing to who you are.
Journey on!

Insight #583

You are not a finished product! You are evolving at the speed of life and each day. Every moment experienced contributes to the total package of YOU!
Journey on!

Insight #584

It's all about you because it begins with you. Your ability to make choices—to care, to give, to be a servant, and to nurture and radiate your talents, skills, and knowledge outward for the benefit of others develops from within.
Journey on!

Contribution

Insight #585

It's all about giving! We are here to assist each other on this incredible journey we call LIFE!
Journey on!

Insight #586

You have your own inner guidance, but so do others. You cannot control people who are on their own journey. Any sharing is a personal choice.
Journey on!

Insight #587

Reach into your inner being each day to find the strength, encouragement, conviction, and guidance to live your purpose, vision, and goals that move you forward in your life's journey.
Journey on!

Insight #588

You only have one life, one opportunity to "get it right." You have one chance for a map, a directional beacon, guidance, inspiration, and to obtain the ability to chart your course to create your "right future" while having a purposeful journey. Be amazing!
Journey on!

Incredible

Insight #589

Feed that inner spirit with positive, uplifting messages to catapult you in the direction of your destiny. Immerse yourself with love, guidance, and direction.
Journey on!

Insight #590

Are you on the right path to make it into your own personal and professional hall of fame? Many athletes put in 40 to 60 hours of work for every one hour in the game. How much time are you investing in your future success?
Journey on!

Insight #591

You desperately need direction, guidance, and strength to make the proper decisions that will continue to move you along your chosen path.
Journey on!

Insight #592

Something is calling and beckoning me to take my journey. Oh yes! It is my future. May I find the strength to make the right choice and heed the call!
Journey on!

Invest

Insight #593

Your journey began the day you were born. There may be many winding turns along with hills and even mountains to climb. However, each step is taking you to a new level and closer to your future.
Journey on!

Insight #594

Reach into your inner being each day to find the strength, encouragement, conviction, and guidance to live your purpose, vision, and goals that move you forward in your life's journey.
Journey on!

Insight #595

Love the life around you for it is all a part of your vision. A portion of everything resides within you.
Journey on!

Insight #596

Feed that inner spirit with positive, uplifting messages to catapult you in the direction of your destiny. Immerse yourself with love, guidance, and proper direction.
Journey on!

Guidance

Insight #597

There will be those you encounter who always seem to point out what you cannot do, your weaknesses, struggles, and faults. Focus on those who point out your strengths, what you are doing right and can build upon. They are the ones who will lift you up to new levels and assist you in achieving your destiny.
Journey on!

Insight #598

Your life is your message to others. What do you radiate outward to all around you? Be amazing! Exude confidence, respect, charm, a positive attitude, victory, joy, and excellence no matter what the circumstances. Be the one who sets the pace. Stay the course and move forward.
Journey on!

Insight #599

As you travel your journey, are you assisting others, lifting them up or tearing them down? Are you pulling others forward or pushing them aside? Remember the "golden rule" and reflect it in your actions.
Journey on!

Insight #600

Don't put all your energy on the negativity, discouragement, and the obstacles before you. Focus on the solutions, the actions required to be positive, confident, and necessary to move you through your storms to your future!
Journey on!

Confidence

Confidence

Be yourself; you don't need anyone's permission.

If you were meant to be controlled, you would have come with a remote.

Awareness Promotes Effectiveness

Fortress or Prison?

Are you creating a fortress or a prison?

Many things cannot be changed, including some people. You are the guardian to your inner spirit, your inner being, your heart. You have the ability to allow or prevent what is coming your way and nurturing your spirit. No one can change your attitude, your peace, without your permission. You are the guard of the bridge to your soul. What and who are you allowing in? You cannot control the actions of others and often cannot change them. However, you can control "YOU" and make the decision to control what you allow in that will fuel your spirit, lift you up, and move you forward.

Are you living in a fortress or have you created a prison? A fortress allows all those good items to come in that will nurture, inspire, and build you up. Yes, you are constantly making decisions as to what you allow in and what may not pass. That constant guard and vigilance is critical for you need that continuous flow of people, ideas, and creativity, for that is the very pulse of life itself. Your choices as to what comes in, what influences and nurtures you, is just as significant. But to not allow that flow, to shut it down, creates a prison where nothing can get in, and you may have a false sense of security, for nothing can get in, but nothing can get out. No growth, no risks, no challenges. You may foolishly feel safe and think you are in a comfort zone, but you simply cannot live, love, develop, change, or move forward. You are in charge of you and decisions must be made. What an incredible responsibility you have before you—the creation of your own right future.

Insight #601

If you are willing to do the work, you can achieve anything!!! There is no sympathy for those who squander their talents. What a poor choice. That's not you. Be amazing! Reach, stretch, and do it! Make the choice to have an abundant life!

Journey on!

Insight #602

Your future is a destination and you must get on board to take the trip! Don't be a "maybe," "someday," or "if-only" person. Be an "I expect," "goal achiever," and "amazing person!" You deserve that, but you must make the choice.

Journey on!

Insight #603

Doubt, fear, no purpose, no direction, goals, or vision will stop you in your tracks. It's time for that to cease. The time for abundance, fulfillment, living your purpose, moving forward, and being amazing is now!

Journey on!

Insight #604

Make the choice to have an incredible attitude. Make it happen. Stay your course and achieve your destiny. Be action-oriented, a doer! Believe that you deserve it. Believe in a soulful bounding leap of abundance.

Journey on!

Encouragement

Insight #605

Whatever it takes, Don't Quit! Double down and charge forward. Win the game of your life!
Journey on!

Insight #606

Mark your thoughts—what you think and embrace will cause you to "Win from Within." Mark your words—what you speak embodies your values and beliefs. Mark your actions—they speak the loudest and reflect all that you are.
Journey on!

Insight #607

Your purpose in life will permeate all that you do. Embrace it: Purpose-Thoughts, Purpose-Dreams, Purpose-Values, Purpose-Beliefs, Purpose-Readings, Purpose-Writings, Purpose-Vision, Purpose-Mission, Purpose-Goals, Purpose-Actions, Purpose-Destiny, Purpose-Journey, Purpose-Right Future!
Journey on!

Insight #608

Have you had your personal revolution yet? The one where you win from within on an individual level before you radiate outward impacting others and attaining even higher levels.
Journey on!

Permeate

Insight #609

Listen well! There are opportunities out there awaiting your discovery. Allow yourself the time to take in your surroundings realizing that your perception may be altered with each step you take. Ah! It's a secret of the universe!
Journey on!

Insight #610

Fear can prevent you from participating fully in life and reaping the benefits you should be receiving. All too often we make choices that prevent or slow down our progress in our journey. Face your fears and confront your future.
Journey on!

Insight #611

You may have walked with greatness and never even realized it. Right next to you may be the very person who will take you through the twist and turns of your journey and on to the next level. Pay attention to those around you and the gifts they possess.
Journey on!

Insight #612

Life teaches you with each step you take that the one constant you can count on is change itself. It often does not take shape as you imagined it would, producing even better results and lifting you higher than imagined. Expect it!
Journey on!

Opportunities

Insight #613

Stop focusing on all that is not happening and turn your attention to the solutions. Take action now; put your energy to use where it will make a difference in moving you forward on your journey.

Journey on!

Insight #614

Be honored each day of your life for the opportunity before you to change, grow, risk, love, and live. Do not be chained to your certitudes for life is meant to be a journey of discovery and awe.

Journey on!

Insight #615

In the blink of an eye your life can change—abundance, promotion, higher levels of achievement than you ever imagined possible. Your life will explode with the force of an active volcano, but it is up to you to direct the flow, radiating it outward in a purposeful way to move you along your chosen course and to your destiny.

Journey on!

Insight #616

Spring, Summer, Fall, and Winter each represents a passage as it draws to an end. However, it also raises awareness of change, renewal, and expectations of things to come. Focus on success, victory, and purposeful actions that will propel you to a new season and the continuation of your journey.

Journey on!

Energy

Insight #617

You will often find yourself at a crossroads. It's easy to feel overwhelmed, frustrated, spent, and defeated. However, when you take that next forward step, suddenly you will realize that your ability to "stay the course" is taking you to victory with renewed strength and energy.

Journey on!

Insight #618

How can your situation possibly work out? The odds seem overwhelmingly against you. Look at how far you have traveled and demonstrate gratitude for the knowledge and skills which have brought you to where you are at. A new "shift" will produce winds to fill your sails, producing new energy to carry you forward.

Journey on!

Insight #619

Your journey may at times look complicated and overwhelming to you. You will be a victor as you confront the obstacles before you. Pay attention to all you do, even the simple things may change your life and move you to that next level.

Journey on!

Insight #620

A new day produces your ability to create opportunities, fresh ideas, and renewed expectations of success. Each day represent another step in the direction of your "right future."

Journey on!

Expectations

Expectations

When opportunity knocks
be sure to answer!

Insight #621

Things will take place along your journey that you are unable to explain. Everything has a purpose and a reason as part of that journey. Carry on!
Journey on!

Insight #622

You will not complete your journey without difficulties, opposition, challenges, and other trials to discourage you. Your breakthrough is taking shape. Don't panic. Do not give in or give up but remain steadfast and carry on!
Journey on!

Insight #623

At first it may seem insurmountable as you begin your journey. However, when you stay the course, with each step you are moving closer to the summit of your mountain. Your effort, purpose, vision, and goals will take you there.
Journey on!

Insight #624

All those you meet along your journey are there to shape you as you travel your path. Yes, that includes not only those you enjoy and who strengthen you, but those who irritate, offend, and appear to drag you down. They each serve a purpose in determining your resolve to carry on!
Journey on!

Shape

Insight #625

It will all come to pass. Your future will unfold in a positive, prosperous, and successful manner. You are about to be fulfilled in ways you never imagined.
Journey on!

Insight #626

At the right time, your truth will be revealed and you will experience an abundance in your life.
Journey on!

Insight #627

Until you are willing to let go of what you have been holding on to as if it were a prize but keeps you from moving forward, you will not expand, grow, risk, change, and live to your fullest. You are the one who must let go to grow!
Journey on!

Insight #628

You have a choice each day to succumb to the negative or to excel. Believe, speak, and expect success, victory, and abundance. For you know that your destiny will not be denied as long as you carry on and have the will to do it!
Journey on!

Prosper

Insight #629

With each step forward, you are being refined, fine-tuned, shaped, molded into a confident, determined individual who will not be satisfied to ever go around anything but to face your challenges head on!

Journey on!

Insight #630

Some things are difficult in your life right now. Stay the course! Learn from those challenges, adjust, and adapt to each situation. It will strengthen you, stretch you, and prepare you for that right future.

Journey on!

Insight #631

Your life, like a river, will run its course long and true. You will properly navigate your course to your future. Do your part to keep moving forward. Your values, faith, and belief will propel you to the fullness of your life.

Journey on!

Insight #632

Don't slow down! Your actions will enable you to conquer the challenge before you.

Journey on!

Molded

Insight #633

It will all come to pass. Your future will unfold in a positive, prosperous, and successful manner. You are about to be fulfilled in ways you never imagined.
Journey on!

Insight #634

A person must take advantage of opportunities as they either present themselves or as they are created. Do it!
Journey on!

Insight #635

The 6 P's—Proper Prior Planning Prevents Poor Performance by Patrick P. Pepper (just made that name up!). Focus and prepare for your future!
Journey on!

Insight #636

There are resources at your disposal along your path. It is your choice to utilize these items and to properly align them so that they work for you on your journey.
Journey on!

Resources

Insight #637

The right challenges, obstacles, individuals, gifts, knowledge, skills, and more are all part of your destiny to create your right future.

Journey on!

Insight #638

Enjoy every step of your journey—each experience, each individual you meet, and each moment of your precious time, for once upon a time never comes again.

Journey on!

Insight #639

Where do you spend your energy and time? It's your choice. You only have so much to give out each day. Be selective and in control of where and who you give to.

Journey on!

Insight #640

Take time for renewal of self. It will sustain you for what lies ahead.

Journey on!

Gifts

Gifts

Insight #641

Guard your heart. Feed your inner spirit with the positive, uplifting, constructive items that will increase you. Do not dwell and give your precious time to those who are negative, tear you down, and are destructive. They steal that which you can never get back.

Journey on!

Insight #642

Your life will unfold when you stay on course and follow your MAP (Make A Plan). It will lead you to your right future.

Journey on!

Insight #643

One of the things that is absolutely necessary is that you have a plan to move you forward each day to achieve your destiny. Then you must work that plan, take action, and be amazing!

Journey on!

Insight #644

Accept where you are at, for it is what it is. However, do not be satisfied or allow yourself to become too comfortable. Where you are at is not where you are staying—your future awaits you. Be amazing!

Journey on!

Constructive

Insight #645

When you understand your purpose and vision for your life, the goals you set each day become so much easier. If they move you forward and reflect your purpose, do it!

Journey on!

Insight #646

It's easy to find fault, be critical, put down, be negative, and bring someone else down. Finding the genius within a person is like finding a buried treasure. Open that vault and let all that hidden wealth come forth.

Journey on!

Insight #647

You can be destroyed from within if you do not control your anger, hatred, and ability to forgive. Be amazing and win from within!

Journey on!

Insight #648

When you feed your inner spirit with favor, increased positive energy, and an abundance of beauty, you will radiate and burst forth to others. You will be amazing because you have created an overflow of love.

Journey on!

Burst

Insight #649

I'd rather go on because there lies my destiny. Anybody can quit when they are feeling challenged, frustrated, or beaten down. It takes courage, determination, and a firm resolve to carry on!

Journey on!

Insight #650

Have the courage to change and do something different! Be amazing! Don't just complain or you will remain where you are. Don't get discouraged. Stay focused and your abundance will come to you.

Journey on!

Insight #651

Don't get discouraged. Stay your course and your abundance will come to you. Stay your course and you will reach your destination.

Journey on!

Insight #652

Your direction, your plan, your map is right there before you—follow it. It will take you to your future!

Journey on!

Resolve

Insight #653

When you are generous with your gifts and freely give to others, you are building bridges of favor, love, faith, goodness, and honor. When you praise, you will amaze!
Journey on!

Insight #654

Fuel your fire and strengthen your foundation with those who will take you to the next level of your journey. That is where your focus of attention needs to be! Continue to move in the direction of your "right future" while having a purposeful journey. Be amazing!
Journey on!

Insight #655

The bounty of positive things in life will come to you the more you share and release your goodness to others. Do not be one who withholds assisting and lifting others up. Release your positive inner thoughts and continuously share them.
Journey on!

Insight #656

Set aside time each day to refresh, refocus, and re-energize your purpose, vision, goals, plan of success, and the course of action you are taking to create your right future!
Journey on!

Honor

Insight #657

With each forward step you take, you are moving into a new version of you. With each step, you are improving, growing, and changing into your life's calling. Will you answer the call? It's for you!

Journey on!

Insight #658

Your future can swoop down upon you without warning, creating chaos and concern, or you can swoop down upon your future with control, with direction, and with purpose.

Journey on!

Insight #659

Take the pledge each and every day to reaffirm your personal commitment to achieve and to continually move forward. Embrace your expectations of self and fulfill your destiny.

Journey on!

Insight #660

Things can feel and appear hopeless, lost, and over. It's not over until you relinquish your authority over self, set your plan aside, and give up. You have the ability to carry on and fulfill your destiny with purpose.

Journey on!

Reaffirm

Reaffirm

Focus your dreams.
If Plan A fails, just remember that you still have 25 letters left.

RE Hollis

Insight #661

Do not dwell on your mistakes. Focus your energy on solutions and your next step. Always have a next step that leads to your future.

Journey on!

Insight #662

Who do you share your talents with? The gifts and skills that you share with others and give freely will return to you in ways you never anticipated. Be amazing!

Journey on!

Insight #663

Restore, refresh, reaffirm, and reclaim your path to success each day. Others may not hear your calling, but you will listen. Others may not see your route or reasons for moving in the direction you have chosen—stay your course, it is your future!

Journey on!

Insight #664

How have you fallen? We all make mistakes and have failures or experience a loss. Your destiny still awaits you and the only thing that can prevent you from getting up, moving forward, and making a positive difference is you!

Journey on!

Reclaim

Insight #665

Slow down at the conclusion of each day. Be pleased with the ground you covered today. Now it is time for renewal and preparing for your next step before it all starts again.

Journey on!

Insight #666

Be honored each day of your life for the opportunity before you to change, grow, risk, live, and love. Do not be chained to your certitudes, for life is meant to be a journey of discovery and awe.

Journey on!

Insight #667

You've gotten yourself in a tight spot. Now is not the time to pull back and be the victim. It's time to pull up all your resources and be a victor.

Journey on!

Insight #668

Do you think that you are going to live forever? Upgrade your goals, step up your actions, and be amazing.

Journey on!

Grow

Insight #669

You are alive and have a new day before you to make a significant difference. Your ability to move forward rests right there within you. Give yourself permission to be amazing!
Journey on!

Insight #670

If you love what you are doing, feel good about it, cherish it, and look forward to it each day. Celebrate! You have discovered your purpose.
Journey on!

Insight #671

Just like a cooking recipe, where the ingredients make all the difference, what you allow yourself to follow, to listen to, touch, feel, take in to your inner spirit will produce who and what you are. It's your choice!
Journey on!

Insight #672

When you have the rug pulled out from under you, you can feel knocked down, abused, ridiculed, heartbroken, and forlorn. Remember that this is an event, a storm, a turbulence that you will pass through. The light of your future lies before you.
Journey on!

Touch

Insight #673

Keep on doing what you know you are meant to do. Follow your charted plan. Stay your course. The results will be even better that what you originally thought.

Journey on!

Insight #674

Feel and express gratitude for all that you encounter along your journey each day. It humbles, softens, and impacts the feelings of your heart.

Journey on!

Insight #675

Find your place to stand and build the right future. You are the architect of your future. Build it strong to achieve the fullness of your destiny.

Journey on!

Insight #676

Do not be judgmental of others on their journey. You know not of their experiences or what they have encountered along their path. Heed your own travels and be amazing. As it is written, "Judge not, lest ye be judged!"

Journey on!

Feel

Insight #677

Failure is an event; it is not who you are. A setback is not the end of your story. There is so much more to be written. It is your choice to make that *setback* a *setup* to catapult you forward.

Journey on!

Insight #678

Be present and accountable at each step in the journey of your life. Be careful not to allow your focus of attention to get lost in all the many distractions that life throws at you.

Journey on!

Insight #679

Realize with all your inner being that you are the difference maker. You are the catalyst that will achieve solutions and produce results. Be amazing!

Journey on!

Insight #680

Surrounding yourself with meaningful, true, positive, uplifting friends who will be vulnerable and honest with you is golden. It will allow you to uncover your own truth.

Journey on!

Catalyst

1,000 Ways in 1,000 Days to Win from Within!

Catalyst

Everyone brings joy to your life.
Some when they enter,
some when they leave.

RE Hollis

Insight #681

It's so easy to be discouraged and stop your journey. Your attitude, your stick-to-itiveness, your passion, and will to do it will be the critical factor.

Journey on!

Insight #682

Miracles happen every single day. Expect them and **M**ake **I**t **R**eally **A** **C**olossal **L**earning **E**xperience—a MIRACLE!

Journey on!

Insight #683

Even now you can make a difference. Impossible simply means you have not found the solution to produce your desired results yet!

Journey on!

Insight #684

Do you have the will to move forward? That's the key! You will take on any foe, accomplish any task, or break down any obstacle to attain your destiny.

Journey on!

Passion

Insight #685

You have the ability to imagine, desire, enthusiastically put into action, and produce meaningful results. Be amazing!
Journey on!

Insight #686

Your vision directs you to where you are going to tomorrow, not just where you are stepping to today. Stay focused on your right future as you move forward.
Journey on!

Insight #687

Start right now! Do it today! Make that critical decision to make a difference and be amazing. It is your choice to step up and into your destiny!
Journey on!

Insight #688

Do not settle for anything that is keeping you from your right future. You are the decision maker and the obstacle breaker to overcome and move forward.
Journey on!

Difference

Insight #689

When you participate in life, make certain that it is with enthusiasm, passion, spirit, drive, determination, and an attitude of humility and gratitude for every single experience. Be amazing!

Journey on!

Insight #690

With each step you take, you make a choice to move forward with love and gratitude or to move off in a direction taking you away from your right future. You make that choice! You reap the results!

Journey on!

Insight #691

Increase your knowledge and skills with each step you take. Think of how glorious the end meaningful results will be.

Journey on!

Insight #692

This is life's journey. One foot in front of the other, always having a next step, always moving forward, ever onward to your destiny. Your path awaits you!

Journey on!

Enthusiasm

Insight #693

Wear your journey well! Every single step was taken with purpose to have you arrive at where you are today. It did not just happen. Move forward in humility and with gratitude for all that has taken place to bring you to this moment in time.
Journey on!

Insight #694

No one has invited you to take the journey you are on. It is your decision, your choice, and your destiny. Realize with your entire being that you would not be where you are today or moving on to your future had you not made that choice. Accept the responsibility you have placed upon yourself.
Journey on!

Insight #695

Just for today, compliment every single individual you encounter or talk about. Focus on the positive, the good, the genius, the honor, the dignity, and respect of that individual. Experience the meaningful results it produces!
Journey on!

Insight #696

The positive habits you develop will lift your steps and move you forward on your path of life.
Journey on!

Accept

Insight #697

Do you stir up others by being negative and bitter? Or, do you protect, honor, respect, and strive to project a positive attitude and spirit of enthusiasm? That will lift you and others up to a higher level and move you forward.

Journey on!

Insight #698

Do not seek vindication for the act of living. Do it right and be fully involved at every turn in the road as you live your amazing journey!

Journey on!

Insight #699

Listen! You know you have made mistakes. Don't repeat them. Shake it off. And know that your purpose will be realized and you will fulfill your destiny.

Journey on!

Insight #700

Because of you, this world is a better place! You are an opportunity for this day to be significant for others. Be the spark that ignites the fire in the hearts of those who will make a positive difference.

Journey on!

Ignite

Ignite

Investing in yourself is like planting an apple tree. You can look forward to future rewards as you both grow.

RE Hollis

Awareness Promotes Effectiveness

It Will Never Be the Same Again!

It will never be the same again! You have taken many steps forward. You have stepped up to a new level of knowledge, skills, and vision. From this new vantage point you have clarity of understanding. All the toils and struggles you have endured are coming to an end. You stand alone at the summit and the view is more than you imagined.

Decisions have to be made. It's not wrong to step away from some involvements if they do not feed your inner spirit. Keep those things that encourage you and move you forward. That which does not should be cast aside, for it discourages and detracts from your true purpose.

How many clubs, groups, or organizations do you belong to? Are they merely a gathering of friends and a social interaction, or are they instruments that truly assist in the achievement of your goals; your destiny? Don't just pass time, for it is too precious to waste. All you do should help to focus your attention on where you are going.

Are you achieving your purpose? Focus everything you have on that which you truly cherish and hold dear to your heart. If you don't know what that is, you are lost and need to be found. You cannot build upon a shaky foundation. Find your place to stand and you will build your right future!

Surround yourself with those who lift you up and encourage your purpose. Encourage and lift up others through your caring and giving.

Insight #701

It all begins with you. Stoke that internal fire with passion, love, and a soulful bounding leap of enthusiasm. Be amazing! That spirit from within will cause you to win!
Journey on!

Insight #702

Be generous, honor others, be kind, caring, and loving, and set out each day realizing the opportunities before you to bring out the genius in each person you encounter on your journey.
Journey on!

Insight #703

Display honor as you travel your path. Pour from your heart the knowledge and skills you have to share and give to others. When you honor others, you are assisting them to discover their own genius that they in turn can share forward.
Journey on!

Insight #704

The real battle is often within you. Your limitations are less than you realize. You hold the key to setting yourself free. Take charge; be amazing! Choose success!
Journey on!

Love

Insight #705

You can feel your destiny and your future deep down within your inner being. Let your passion release that heart power to take you to the next level. That dream requires your belief, your enthusiasm, and your decision to act for it to become your reality.

Journey on!

Insight #706

You are only one break, one pivot point, one degree of change, one decision, one moment in time away from activating and releasing all that you have expected all along. Make it happen!

Journey on!

Insight #707

Choose to stay focused. Choose to carry on! Choose to not allow any challenge or any obstacle to keep you from your destiny.

Journey on!

Insight #708

Have the courage to live a life that is true to your inner being and not the external voices shouting at you. What are your expectations of yourself? Live up to them!

Journey on!

Decision

Insight #709

Please realize that you will never succeed in every endeavor alone. Do not hesitate to seek out help from those you know, like, trust, admire, and respect.

Journey on!

Insight #710

Be grateful for all those who have made the journey before you and perhaps cleared the path of some obstacles you do not have to confront as a result of their efforts.

Journey on!

Insight #711

Your concerns, frustration, problems, debts, health concerns, direction, struggles, relationships, sadness, and failures are all about to change. An abundance that you have never even imagined is about to lift off and catapult you to a new level of achievement, solutions, increase, renewed health, a charted course of action, happiness, and success.

Journey on!

Insight #712

Your true happiness will emerge from within you. It will radiate outward to light your path.

Journey on!

Happiness

Insight #713

If you do not believe that you can accomplish your task, then move out of the way, for someone else will be moving ahead with it. Give yourself permission to do it!
Journey on!

Insight #714

You will encounter so much on your journey. What an incredible learning experience it is. Remember (and this is one of the most challenging items for many to accept and embrace) that you are inescapably responsible for your own actions and the consequences of those actions.
Journey on!

Insight #715

Your failures will not hold you down because you will see them as learning opportunities. Forgive yourself. You do not need to suffer with your mistakes. Trust yourself and move on!
Journey on!

Insight #716

Rejoice in your victories, learn from failures and things that caused you to wander off your path, and give gratitude for all you have accomplished. Okay! Now what's your "next step" to move toward your "right future?"
Journey on!

Rejoice

Insight #717

There should be times when you "pull yourself in", relax, energize, and refocus all that you are about. It will keep you on that right course to your future.
Journey on!

Insight #718

The past should not be an excuse for a poor future. Give up all hope of a better past and move on, look forward, and create that right future!
Journey on!

Insight #719

Life is so exciting with all its joys and tears, challenges, and success. All you encounter as you travel your journey contribute to the wholeness that is you!
Journey on!

Insight #720

You've got one shot at life. You can't afford to waste your precious time. Do things with a purposeful intent and be amazing!
Journey on!

Refocus

Refocus

Stay focused on your Life's Journey with positive thoughts.

RE Hollis

Insight #721

You may focus on regrets, frustrations, mistakes, and disappointments if that is your choice. However, what purpose will it serve? Move forward! Joy and enthusiasm for life is up to you!

Journey on!

Insight #722

Your growth in knowledge and skills will continue your entire life with your permission. Open that door and take it all in! Never think you have "arrived" and that there is nothing more to learn.

Journey on!

Insight #723

There is abundance, celebration, and new levels of achievement to be accomplished. However, it is up to you to have it come to pass. Be amazing!

Journey on!

Insight #724

Jump in! Participate with all your "heart power," love, and spirit! Your enthusiasm and positive attitude will elevate you to new levels of success.

Journey on!

Responsible

Insight #725

It will never be exactly like it used to be. However, with the proper attitude, action, and decision to move forward, it will be better than you ever imagined.
Journey on!

Insight #726

Go back and change yesterday please. What, you can't?! Then why are you living there? Live where you can make a difference and that is right now, right here, today! That will impact your future.
Journey on!

Insight #727

Let others hear your appreciation and gratitude for them. It adds to the hope, love, and optimism that propel you forward.
Journey on!

Insight #728

Give your body the natural time it requires for healing, strength, energy, and optimal performance. Your best medicine is peaceful sleep at the end of a productive day.
Journey on!

Optimism

Insight #729

Are you truly focusing your attention? There is so much you think you have to do, but your attention should be focusing on those things you actually need to do.

Journey on!

Insight #730

The power of controlling your thoughts is key in allowing yourself to win from within. What you feed your inner being with will nurture your very spirit and the result will radiate out to others.

Journey on!

Insight #731

Do not shy away from the challenges, the obstacles, and all that lies before you. Step forward and be the amazing person you are.

Journey on!

Insight #732

Proper planning and preparation behind the scenes is so important to the final result. Your time and effort will pay off many times over for you. Abundance awaits you. Be amazing!

Journey on!

Power

Insight #733

If you dwell on I can't, I won't, if only, I'm weak, I'll never be able to, you have already set yourself up for defeat. I can, I will, I'm strong, I will do whatever it takes to move forward and succeed, you will. You decide, choose your words, your thoughts, and your actions carefully. They chart your course of action.
Journey on!

Insight #734

As you move forward on your journey, be certain to assist others in locating their place to stand and giving them the opportunity to move forward as well.
Journey on!

Insight #735

What you are today is the result of each step you have taken in the direction of your chosen destiny. Think, ask, and decide where each step is taking you. Then move forward in confidence.
Journey on!

Insight #736

If it builds you up, makes you a better person, and will influence you in a positive, uplifting manner, do it! If it will tear you down, detract from whom you want to be, and is a negative influence, don't do it! It's a blinding flash of the obvious.
Journey on!

Choose

Insight #737

Set your mind and stay focused on the course you have set for yourself. That is the direction you will move in as long as you stay focused.

Journey on!

Insight #738

If you are making your choices willingly, then it is not so much a sacrifice but a reflection of the passion in your life.

Journey on!

Insight #739

You make choices every single day of your life that will move you in the direction of your right future or move you away from that desired direction. It is up to you. The choice is yours.

Journey on!

Insight #740

You have made it so far already on your journey. Now take that next step and fulfill your destiny. You are the only one that this particular journey has been mapped out for. It will take you to your right future!

Journey on!

Permit

Permit

Take the "right" road to memorable.
Let the average be "left" behind.

RE Hollis

Insight #741

As you build your inner being, there are times you have to adjust your erroneous conscience as you learn and increase awareness as to what is right, necessary, proper, and just!
Journey on!

Insight #742

Give yourself something to talk about. Be amazing! Startle yourself each day as to how much you have accomplished and how far you have traveled on your journey!
Journey on!

Insight #743

Don't forget your daily pledge to your success. This will cause you to focus and to expect all that is to be. If it takes root in your spirit, it will ignite your reality.
Journey on!

Insight #744

It may be difficult at times to seek the genius in each individual. For some, we may have to look a bit further, but find it you will. When you do, it will alter your life!
Journey on!

Conscience

Insight #745

Let people who are important to you know that they are important and play a significant role in who you are. It's a beautiful thing to do and it produces joy!

Journey on!

Insight #746

Expect good, positive things to overtake and surprise you on your journey. This is your moment in time—your life's journey. Expect fulfillment and abundance.

Journey on!

Insight #747

One way to avoid loneliness is to surround yourself with those whom you share much in common and who feed your inner spirit in a positive, meaningful way.

Journey on!

Insight #748

Do not lose your expectancy. You have come so far and your journey will not only continue, it will be completed! Promises, dreams, hopes, and desires will come to pass. Expect it!

Journey on!

Importance

Insight #749

Quit it! Stop making excuses. It's easy to get off course, go the wrong way, and complicate your life. Take action! Do it now and don't look back. Be amazing!
Journey on!

Insight #750

Do you have the right frame of mind to put you in the right place, at the right time, for the right reasons? It will happen if you open and walk through those doors of opportunity.
Journey on!

Insight #751

Allow yourself to have a balanced life. It will lend to overall health. When you binge and purge, it detracts from the meaningful results you desire to achieve. Get off that roller coaster existence—have a smooth ride!
Journey on!

Insight #752

It is time to be healthy and whole. This is your moment! Be a prisoner of expectation! Have your mind properly set to be focused and to take action!
Journey on!

Balance

Insight #753

How are you spending your precious time as you are moving at the speed of life? Are you creating your own right future while having a purposeful journey?

Journey on!

Insight #754

When you know you are doing that which is right, necessary, proper, and just, you will move forward with confidence. That will strengthen your resolve and fulfill your destiny.

Journey on!

Insight #755

There is favor in your life. You have all the tools and skills in your possession to make it happen. Only you can do it. Be amazing, be bold, and take the actions that will move you forward.

Journey on!

Insight #756

Noise, distractions, and a bombardment of sensory overload await you each day along your path. Take a pause, collect your thoughts, focus your vision, and then carry on and move forward to your future.

Journey on!

Necessary

Insight #757

You need those who believe and are joined in your beliefs, vision, purpose, and spirit. They will energize and move you onward. Put those others out of your life, for they detract and do not add to your fulfillment.

Journey on!

Insight #758

Everywhere you travel, you bring an advantage to each step on your journey. Only you can bring the uniqueness, the genius, and the wonder of you. Bring it, share it, and allow that amazing you to radiate forth!

Journey on!

Insight #759

Don't be shy. Ask, ask, ask for that which will compliment, increase you, and raise you to that next level of success. Do not accept where you are, but accept your destiny and move on to where you are going!

Journey on!

Insight #760

Pivot, turn around, and look at things with a new perspective and realize that one small change can make all the difference in your life.

Journey on!

Advantage

Advantage

B is for Belief

If you believe you can't,
    you won't.
If you believe you can,
    you will.

RE Hollis

Insight #761

Every day is another beginning. Every day you have a choice to invest or withdraw from your own charted course. Make the choice to move forward.

Journey on!

Insight #762

You have been chosen for this journey. Is it well spent and purposefully focused on your destiny? Don't look back five, ten or more years from now in disappointment because you were not tuned in to the right channel.

Journey on!

Insight #763

You cannot spend your time in the chicken coop and expect to soar with eagles. Be with those that you aspire to be like. Choose wisely, for it will reflect upon your success and the level you attain.

Journey on!

Insight #764

Keep your thoughts, actions, and inner spirit all in sync and linked together to move you in a positive, on-course direction. Nothing will be able to stand before you and block you from your destiny.

Journey on!

Beginning

Insight #765

What is about to happen is far beyond what you ever imagined. You will attain your expectations as a result of your efforts, determination, perseverance, focus, purpose, vision, and goals. Your future is about to embrace you!

Journey on!

Insight #766

Disappointments are inevitable, but misery is optional. Do not tolerate that which you do not want to be. Invest your precious time in that which will lift you up to the levels you are striving for.

Journey on!

Insight #767

Who is in your inner circle? People who support, believe, move you, promote, lift you, and push you forward? Why would you be doing things any other way? Your time is so precious and you should move forward each day in a purposeful manner.

Journey on!

Insight #768

Do not give up, give in, quit, stop, or turn around. Stay your course, keep stepping forward, and stay focused on that directional beacon moving you to your right future.

Journey on!

Efforts

Insight #769

Others will attempt to distract you, knock you off your charted course, and take you from your purposeful journey. Do not give in to them! Stay the course!

Journey on!

Insight #770

We will all fall down, become discouraged, lose hope, and not know which way to turn. This is where you call upon your purpose, vision, and goals to give you the strength to carry on. Draw from them the guidance, determination, resolve to rise up, and focus on that directional beacon to move forward!

Journey on!

Insight #771

Step forward and step up to a new level of success. Sing a new song, put a new step in your walk, and let your face display your confidence.

Journey on!

Insight #772

We are living in a time where there are so many struggles. It is imperative to know your purpose and direction in order to stay on course in life. Reinforce your focus each day. Pledge to commit to the path that will move you forward.

Journey on!

Display

Insight #773

No one else does your job in exactly the way you do. Your combination of skills, talents, and attitude make your situation unique and unlike any other.
Journey on!

Insight #774

Don't allow the contradictions found in your life to keep you from your destiny. Within a weakness or a frustration may be found that very strength to carry on.
Journey on!

Insight #775

A requirement is that you stop all those behaviors that have been holding you down. Release them and then release yourself to the opportunities that lie before you.
Journey on!

Insight #776

Some people will never change. You have control over *you* and that is where it all begins. Make the difference, be the change you seek, draw from your inner strength, and do it!
Journey on!

Behaviors

Insight #777

Do not let your fears get the best of you. They can divert you from your chosen path, taking on a life of their own. Confront your fears and move forward to your destiny.
Journey on!

Insight #778

All your travels, the roadblocks, hills, mountains, valleys, and storms have not been a limitation to slow you down but a learning experience to inspire and encourage you, giving you the ability to move forward.
Journey on!

Insight #779

Stretch yourself! Get out of that comfort zone and test your metal. You will be astounded at all you are able to accomplish!
Journey on!

Insight #780

Do not stop. Do not place your life on hold. Tap into your energy and make the choice right here, right now, to act! You will not achieve that next level by staying where you are. Start climbing!
Journey on!

Climb

Climb

Life's Journey is like a road map—no directions, you get to choose.

RE Hollis

#781

Worry causes you to go around in meaningless circles of doubt and inactivity. Be concerned, but carry on, take action, and be amazing!

Journey on!

Insight #782

The will to do it, the skills to shape it, and the proper positive attitude are all required elements for success. With these, you move forward with confidence.

Journey on!

Insight #783

Others are not pouring misery on you. It is a choice you yourself have made. Stop sitting around in it and take the actions required to change your situation.

Journey on!

Insight #784

You have beautiful, kind, victorious, giving, positive thoughts within you. Only you can release them and bring them to the surface to become your reality.

Journey on!

Positive

Insight #785

Be intimate with life. Embrace it, love it, exhaust it. You will move to levels you never even imagined!
Journey on!

Insight #786

Your mind, thoughts, inner being, and spirit are what radiate outward and direct your life and observable behavior. That is where it all begins. What are you thinking?
Journey on!

Insight #787

Be totally transparent with your own self. Only then can you find your place to stand and begin to build your right future.
Journey on!

Insight #788

When you are down in the depths of despair, that is the time to call upon and depend on your inner spirit to guide you back to the correct path. Listen well and act!
Journey on!

Transparent

Insight #789

Quit discounting yourself. It slows you down. Get out of your own way and decide to be the amazing individual that you are.
Journey on!

Insight #790

Some of the greatest lessons you will learn in life will come out of failures, losses, frustrations, and diversions. They strengthen your resolve and determination to achieve.
Journey on!

Insight #791

Stir up your life. Shake up and encourage yourself daily with words that feed your inner spirit and keep you focused on that directional beacon to your future.
Journey on!

Insight #792

You are alive, vibrant, and ready to move in the direction of your right future. Give yourself permission to open the door and walk on to your destiny.
Journey on!

Vibrant

Insight #793

You cannot go it alone. Identify those who will strengthen, lift, and help you rise to higher levels. Their positive qualities will have a significant impact upon who you are and all you will become.

Journey on!

Insight #794

Be content but not satisfied. In other words, enjoy your surroundings with each step you are taking on your journey. That will provide you with the ability to capitalize on where you are at any given moment in time.

Journey on!

Insight #795

Those who lift you up and move you forward are sharpening your talents and skills. Embrace them, for they are part of the team you want to move, step forward, and upward with.

Journey on!

Insight #796

Are you being defeated or developed? What you need to survive and thrive is right there before you. Embrace your destiny and take action.

Journey on!

Qualities

Insight #797

While focusing on that "golden ring" in your life, remember to appreciate that which you have right now. Your positive attitude allows you to grow and move to that next level.

Journey on!

Insight #798

Let go of those who are holding you back. If they will not embrace and support your purpose, vision, and goals, you should part company with them, for they are holding you back from your destiny.

Journey on!

Insight #799

You are where you are supposed to be. Right now, right here, at this moment in time things are taking place that are absolutely necessary for the next portion of your journey. Make it count! Realize that you are where you are for a purpose—embrace it!

Journey on!

Insight #800

No matter where you are on your journey, the one absolute thing that will carry you on is love. That is the tie that binds it all together. The struggles, the stressors, the challenges, the good times, and the celebrations all are interdependently glued together with love. There lies your joy.

Journey on!

Supposed

Supposed

Life is like a camera:
focus on what is important,
capture the good times,
develop from the negatives,
and if things don't work out,
take another shot.

RE Hollis

Awareness Promotes Effectiveness

Life is a Puzzle!

Picture a jigsaw puzzle with over 5,000 pieces. There are no instructions; no picture of what it will look like when finished. Yet you begin to piece it together.

And then it happens!

There is elation and joy when you discover a few of the components that fit together and you are encouraged to go on, hour after hour, day after day. Celebrate those moments!

And then it happens!

There are many frustrating moments when nothing seems to fit or make sense and you consider flipping over the entire table upon which it rests. But you don't. You calm down, you refocus, you get back to work. And ever so slowly, it starts to come together. Celebrate those moments!

And then it happens!

There are even milestones where suddenly you feel unstoppable! A huge portion of the pieces connect as if by magic. You don't even understand how it happened. Joyous moments and then you go on. After many long hours and days, it is beginning to shape up, to form an image. All these many seemingly unrelated parts now have a meaningful purpose. You stay on course, driven to achieve the end result. You are beginning to have a vision, a mission that shouts you will not be deprived of or deterred from your destiny. Celebrate those moments!

And then it happens!

Someone or something bumps the table, rocks your world, and many of the pieces and parts are flung asunder, hither and yon, helter skelter. Some even falling completely off the table. Some are a bit battered and bruised. You pick them up, step back for a moment to re-energize, and get back at it with even more of a renewed drive and zeal than originally existed—more than you even realized or imagined you ever had. Oh the joy! More focused, you persevere and are determined and confident that you will achieve your goal. You will be victorious. Celebrate those moments!

And then, it happens!

You hold the final few pieces in the palm of your hand. You already know the answer. You can see the final picture. You have achieved clarity of understanding. You place those final pieces into the puzzle and gaze upon the final total package.

It is a picture of YOU!—unique, amazing, beautiful, and whole!

Insight #801

Walk, run, soar with those who will lift you to those high levels you aspire to. Choose companions, colleagues, friends, who will assist you in embracing your destiny.

Journey on!

Insight #802

Rise higher, step forward and step up with each movement you take. Appreciate each level and each step taken on the ladder to your destiny.

Journey on!

Insight #803

There is so much sensory bombardment. You live in a social media society filled with many illusions. Do not lose your focus of attention and grasp on your true reality.

Journey on!

Insight #804

All things must pass! Transitions will take place. Some, you will never quite grasp with complete understanding. However, each of these is moving you to your destiny.

Journey on!

Aspire

Insight #805

How do you leverage your life's journey? Remember that it was Archimedes who stated, "If I could find my place to stand with the proper lever and fulcrum, I could move the world." Move your world!

Journey on!

Insight #806

Just when everything seems to be doing well, life will throw you another curveball. Embrace it and make it work for you as a tool to take you from your comfort zone to your discover zone.

Journey on!

Insight #807

Get out of my way! I will achieve my destiny and move to that next level. No obstacle or challenge will keep me from my purposeful journey.

Journey on!

Insight #808

Each morning, renew that inner fire and allow it to burn brightly so that you will radiate your spirit outwardly in the actions you display. Be amazing!

Journey on!

Leverage

Insight #809

Look at the big picture of your life. By all means, make it a fascinating journey that only you can take. You are constantly making choices to move you forward.
Journey on!

Insight #810

Shake things up, make a difference, get out of your comfort zone, stretch, grow, and be amazing! Only you can give yourself permission to make this happen.
Journey on!

Insight #811

If you didn't have to deal with the pain, discomfort, and frustrations before you, the necessary changes you must experience in achieving that next level may not happen.
Journey on!

Insight #812

Don't get so wrapped up in doing so much that you lose your ability and grasp on intimacy with life. It takes courage and determination to live life to its fullest.
Journey on!

Fascinating

Insight #813

Greater levels of fulfillment, joy, growth, increase, and promotion are all awaiting you as you move through your difficulties, challenges, and trials you are confronting.

Journey on!

Insight #814

All you are experiencing is preparing you for the next level and fulfilling your purpose. That pushing, carrying, and lifting is serving a purpose as each moves you forward.

Journey on!

Insight #815

Often, what you think is the worst thing that might happen turns out to be the very thing that causes you to stretch, grow, and adapt to the changes before you.

Journey on!

Insight #816

The fact that you don't "fit in" with those who do not support you, lift you up, encourage, and push you forward is actually an asset and a compliment to your own personal focus, determination, and commitment.

Journey on!

Apt

Insight #817

Don't be depressed with changes taking place. They are serving a necessary purpose in taking you to your next level. Accept where you are but expect to move forward!
Journey on!

Insight #818

Get a grip and a grasp on each item that comes your way during your journey. Embrace the good and the bad, the total package of all life offers. Each serves a purpose in promoting you to that next level of success.
Journey on!

Insight #819

You are the result of every single experience your journey presents to you—the good and the bad, the positive and the negative. They each serve a purpose in your development and movement to that next level.
Journey on!

Insight #820

You are going to face some tough, challenging, frustrating times. It is not a setback but a setup for future success. Each step serves a purpose in your journey.
Journey on!

Challenging

Challenging

Perseverance—
   Get knocked down 6,
   get up 7.

RE Hollis

Insight #821

There's no second show! Your Life's Journey happens once! It's happening right now! Make it memorable. Embrace it. Live it!
Journey on!

Insight #822

Who shouts out for you and cheers you on? Who has your back? Who can you fall back on for encouragement, support, and a positive affirmation that you are on course? Identify and embrace that individual. We need each other to complete the journey.
Journey on!

Insight #823

You may not understand all that you are going through on the way to your destiny. Don't try to avoid these things, but go out to meet them. As you deal with each situation, you are moving closer to your future.
Journey on!

Insight #824

Your path invites you and beckons you to your future, but you must step up and into that which will fulfill your destiny. Do what is right, necessary, proper, and just. The decisions you make will propel or repel your efforts to move forward.
Journey on!

Memorable

Insight #825

Plan the perfect trip—the journey of your life. You're all set. You have the tools, knowledge, and skills along with the attitude, caring, and determination. You have a ticket. You've made the reservations. Go now!
Journey on!

Insight #826

You have not finished writing that next chapter of your life. Many adventures lie ahead for you. It is not over. You are still moving forward and still powerful. Your enthusiasm, spirit, energy, determination, attitude, and will to do it will prevail.
Journey on!

Insight #827

A soulful bounding leap, a breakthrough, a new level are all awaiting you as you move forward. Take that next step!
Journey on!

Insight #828

A great bounding leap is to take place for you. Let go of all those things that have been holding you down and out. Your destiny is coming and brings a lifting energy to propel you to new levels.
Journey on!

Bounding

Insight #829

At long last your dreams are being realized. The effort and precious time you have invested have all made the difference. Celebrate and dance to the music of your life!
Journey on!

Insight #830

You will finish all that you have started. Unexpected wondrous items will take place that will pave a way to your destiny. Those dreams you have cherished for so long are being revitalized and in alignment with the directional beacon showing the path to your future.
Journey on!

Insight #831

More than anything you possess is the will to do it! That confidence, determination, courage, and perseverance will lead you to your destiny.
Journey on!

Insight #832

Don't lose your passion. Even the difficult times serve a purpose. You will grow, learn, develop, and stretch to success and fulfillment. Allow each experience to be significant.
Journey on!

Investment

Insight #833

Get off that merry-go-round that is causing you to move in circles. Move forward, stay your course!

Journey on!

Insight #834

Look at the choices you have made. That is what has taken you to where you are right now in your journey. Choose wisely as you carry on!

Journey on!

Insight #835

You have come a long way on your journey. Don't forget to reach out and assist others as they strive to achieve higher levels.

Journey on!

Insight #836

It all begins with your thinking. If you believe you are defeated, then you already are. When you tell yourself you can't, then you surely won't. Feed your inner spirit each day with messages that are healthy, strong, confident, determined, and successful!

Journey on!

Messages

Insight #837

Periodically take in all the beautiful sounds around you: a special song, music that lifts your spirit, the sound of another's voice, a thunderstorm, animals, and birds. These are sounds that heal and raise us up.

Journey on!

Insight #838

Clarity of understanding does not just happen. The search and the quest to carry on, moving in the right direction, is worthy of your focused attention.

Journey on!

Insight #839

Remember the excitement and enthusiasm you had for life as a child. It's still there and only you can reclaim it. It is the fire of your very passion. Turn it on, turn it up, and be amazing!

Journey on!

Insight #840

You are inescapably responsible for you and each action you allow yourself to take. Be aware of that power you possess and how important each decision you make is.

Journey on!

Music

1,000 Ways in 1,000 Days to Win from Within!

Music

Life's Journey
The bridge from what
if to what is!

RE Hollis

Insight #841

When you trust yourself to do and be all you are truly capable of, watch out, for you have unleashed the power of an active volcano. Be amazing!
Journey on!

Insight #842

Every step you take in that right direction moves you closer to your destiny. You always have a next step within you. Take it!
Journey on!

Insight #843

Maintenance of self on a regular basis is a basic building block to success. If you don't take care of you, how can you possibly be prepared for all that lies before you?
Journey on!

Insight #844

The love and the passion you have for life is a gift. You decide where it is to be shared. This is not something you can buy. However, it is yours to give, and it is priceless.
Journey on!

Maintenance

Insight #845

When your inner being is talking, are you ready to listen and take it in? This is your passion, your enthusiasm for life, charting your course of action. Listen well!

Journey on!

Insight #846

Your fears can stop you in your tracks if you allow them to take control. Remember that it is your choice to confront and deal with these roadblocks to your destiny.

Journey on!

Insight #847

Declutter your life. When you remain focused on your purpose, your vision, and your goals, there is little room for useless items that detract from your creativity.

Journey on!

Insight #848

When you know where you are going and your determination is unflappable, nothing will keep you from your charted course of action.

Journey on!

Declutter

Insight #849

Allow yourself to feel and experience the emotions of the human side of life. After all, we are not perfect beings but human beings.

Journey on!

Insight #850

Renew your purpose each morning with your spirit from within reminding you where you are going and the beautiful future that awaits you. Then get busy!

Journey on!

Insight #851

Your life story has many chapters. Some are challenging, perhaps even scary and unnerving. However, there are more stories in the book of your life to be written. Your destiny will come to pass.

Journey on!

Insight #852

Live a life of purpose that reflects your values, goals, and vision. Guilt on the inside will prevent glorious things radiating from within you to the outside.

Journey on!

Glorious

Insight #853

How long will your journey be? How many steps forward will you take in order to achieve your destiny? Your future awaits!
Journey on!

Insight #854

Love, kindness, and caring are embraced by those with a passion, purpose, and vision. Others move away confused, lost and with no sense of direction. Love is the answer!
Journey on!

Insight #855

Whatever is holding you back, whatever guilt or heaviness weighs you down, it is time to let go. Break those chains and move forward. You will not change the past, but the future awaits you.
Journey on!

Insight #856

Don't be consumed by negativity and lies. You (as we all) have failed at some point. We are not perfect beings. Forgive yourself and stop being a victim of your past. Be victorious in your future!
Journey on!

Journey

Insight #857

When a building is under construction, the pylons are driven deep into the earth to create a firm foundation to hold that structure. Drive your pylons deep to build upon and take you to the completion of your journey.

Journey on!

Insight #858

Your path contains many detours; roads that go off in directions that are not your true course. It's easy to become discouraged. The significant difference in this journey is "You!" Stay the course!

Journey on!

Insight #859

Like a heavy winter coat—take it off and remove all that holds you back from your destiny. Only you can shed those shackles and move to a higher level. It's your choice!

Journey on!

Insight #860

Who do you trust who can assist you on your journey? You need to share, communicate, and discuss your concerns, goals, purpose, and vision. Then give yourself permission to act!

Journey on!

Foundation

Foundation

If you look like success,
walk like success,
and talk like success,
you will be a success.

RE Hollis

Insight #861

It's important to pause, reflect, remember, and have gratitude for all who guide, coach, mentor, teach, and provide assistance to you throughout your journey.

Journey on!

Insight #862

Do you have the proper attitude to step up and achieve your next level of success? You own it and no one else can change it without your permission. The choice is yours!

Journey on!

Insight #863

Get back up! So you've had a tough time, suffered a loss, been discouraged. Get up and honor your life and others by continuing on your journey.

Journey on!

Insight #864

Get back up! So you've had a tough time, suffered a loss, been discouraged. Get up and honor your life and others by continuing on your journey.

Journey on!

Mentor

Insight #865

Don't be too busy to nurture intimacy. It is the reflection of your life's passion with people, projects, events, places, and moments in time. Embrace it!

Journey on!

Insight #866

When you are unable to focus on something you believe in, take a moment to step back and reflect. Why are you doing this? How does it compliment your purpose? Where will it take you? Perhaps it is not right and a change is in order.

Journey on!

Insight #867

Life in all of its splendor will also present moments of loss. It's important to know how you will deal with these times. Grief is a process. Who will you turn to? How will your inner spirit assist and guide you?

Journey on!

Insight #868

Do not ever lose your humor. It provides a light when things look bleak. Being able to laugh in the face of adversity can provide a bonding agent for you and others to carry on!

Journey on!

Compliment

Insight #869

Stop blaming others for your own actions and decisions. Accept responsibility for you along with the consequences of your actions. Be amazing!

Journey on!

Insight #870

Today may be the single most significant learning experience of your entire life, so far! It is an opportunity for abundance and moving in the direction of your future.

Journey on!

Insight #871

Live your life through your own eyes. Experience and appreciate every moment and focus on the gift of your life.

Journey on!

Insight #872

Have a fantastic journey! And why not? You are the pilot of your plane, charting your course, altitude, aptitude, and attitude. You will rise to heights you have never even imagined.

Journey on!

Consequences

Insight #873

You will have disappointments, losses, hard times, and challenges. Hard to imagine, but that is normal and necessary as you regain and restore your footing to carry on!
Journey on!

Insight #874

Be prepared for all that life will present to you. Each experience, good or bad, is setting you up for achievement, success, and victory. Embrace each moment and learn from it.
Journey on!

Insight #875

Stop complaining—start obtaining! Use that energy to achieve and move forward. Those challenges you are facing are refining and shaping you for greater things that lie ahead. Learn!
Journey on!

Insight #876

Yes, you are different as a result of your own unique experiences. Capitalize on that! It is your strength and only you can release it.
Journey on!

Obtaining

Insight #877

Your promised land is your right future. Continue to step forward and upwards to your destiny. Each step takes you away from your frustrations, disappointments, obstacles, and those attempting to hold you back. Stay the course!
Journey on!

Insight #878

Who do you trust? Who do you allow yourself to be vulnerable with? Those people are priceless and will assist you on your journey with truth, encouragement, and love.
Journey on!

Insight #879

Who are the functional people in your life? Embrace them. They will assist you on your incredible journey. Separate yourself from those who are dysfunctional, for they will hold you back from all your destiny intends for you.
Journey on!

Insight #880

What is projecting outward that comes from the inside of your soul? Isn't that what really matters and should be guiding you to your destiny?
Journey on!

Vulnerable

Vulnerable

Information is not knowledge. What you *do* with information becomes knowledge.

RE Hollis

Insight #881

If you are not where you want to be, you are not fighting back enough. You are capable of more. Allow your inner spirit and strength to move you to that next level in your quest.

Journey on!

Insight #882

Who knew that it was going to all work out? You did and it was the result of your hard work, perseverance, and determination. Carry on!

Journey on!

Insight #883

Today is the day. Now is your time. This is the moment to make a difference, tackle the obstacles in your life, work your goals, take action, and move forward.

Journey on!

Insight #884

Enjoy a balanced life, a total package of wholeness—psychological, family, financial, fitness, transitional, relaxation, outdoors, and nutritional, to name a few. It all impacts your total wellness!

Journey on!

Quest

Insight #885

In order to properly identify and move forward purposefully, you need to know those values you personally embrace. They will guide you to your right future.

Journey on!

Insight #886

Sometimes your most productive moments can come right after you give yourself permission to take a break or pause. It promotes reflection and time to refocus upon that which is most important.

Journey on!

Insight #887

When you master the ability to truly focus your attention to where it needs to be, you will experience a calming effect. It is like being in the eye of the storm.

Journey on!

Insight #888

The significance of the choices we have made along our journey will often not be realized for some time, even years. However, the meaning will eventually be revealed as we stay our course.

Journey on!

Calming

Insight #889

Periodically stop and listen to that inner voice calling and directing you. It will guide you to win from within!
Journey on!

Insight #890

It is very difficult to recognize, define, and celebrate your own uniqueness when it is confined to the boundaries established by others. Build your own future!
Journey on!

Insight #891

You will reach the fullness of your destiny, but it will not be without some purposeful struggles. They will bend, shape, mold, strengthen, and enlighten you so that you may move forward.
Journey on!

Insight #892

It's a very long journey, so be selective as to who will join you on your travels. Will they assist you, guide you, and stay with you through the good and the challenging times? If so, be honored to call them friend.
Journey on!

Build

Insight #893

Move cautiously with each step you take as you move forward to achieve each new level in your life. Be focused on your continued growth. Each decision, each action, will produce meaningful results for you.

Journey on!

Insight #894

Do not keep doing the same things over and over again that are moving you away from your destiny. Embrace the challenge and take the actions that will raise you to your next level of success.

Journey on!

Insight #895

What part of life do you encourage and grow? Just as adding more wood to a fire keeps it burning bright, so, too, the actions you choose are feeding the results you desire.

Journey on!

Insight #896

Stop talking yourself out of seeing the truth. It might just be a coincidence and the sun might rise in the west. Do you have clarity of understanding, purpose, vision, and the ability to take action?

Journey on!

Coincidence

Insight #897

You are an ongoing process of continuous improvement. Each day, you make that choice to move forward to achieve an abundant life of success with personal and professional wholeness.

Journey on!

Insight #898

Start your day in control of your feelings, emotions, and desires. You are in control of you if you so choose. Choose your path, your direction, your actions. That will take you to your destiny.

Journey on!

Insight #899

You will not understand all you struggle with on your journey. However, you can learn, grow, and go on. Do not waste your struggles. Turn them into a force to move you forward.

Journey on!

Insight #900

Are you looking at the "big picture" of your life or only focused on the here and now? Chart your course with the end in mind. Each step should move you to your next level of success.

Journey on!

Force

Force

Batter up!

You don't have to be great to start, but you have to start to be great.

RE Hollis

Awareness Promotes Effectiveness

Your Perception of Self!

Your perception of self sets the boundaries of your life.

Only with your permission can others diminish your authority, honor, joy, and take away your dreams. When you know and embrace your purpose , you will stay your course and no one will deter you.

In order to remain on course, you must maintain your vision. Your purposeful journey requires your focus of attention. You will be confident and secure in your own person when you stay set on your directional beacon.

Who supports you, raises you up, and assists you in attaining each new level in your Journey? Surround and embrace those individuals. They realize the strength and determination of purpose that you possess, your deep commitment to your vision and goals, the spirit from within that drives you on, and they are there to remind you who you are.

Do not be mediocre. A true master never gets too comfortable and is never satisfied. Keep reaching for your dreams. They will become your reality!

Insight #901

Your pain is a sign that a change is taking place. Focus on where it is taking you: a new level, a step in the direction of your right future, a significant learning experience. You will never be the same!

Journey on!

Insight #902

Are you controlled by your feelings or your reason? Your inner spirit will guide you in making the right choices even in difficult times.

Journey on!

Insight #903

Other events may overshadow your plans. Do not lose your focus, your purpose, the course you have charted to your future. Remain true to your course.

Journey on!

Insight #904

Are you able to see the big picture? Each step is a portion of the master plan that forms your right future. As you move forward, your map and your charted course become crystal clear.

Journey on!

Change

Insight #905

Every single day and night throughout your entire journey, give your all: your passion, your spirit, and enthusiasm. It is what dreams are made of, and they will produce your reality.
Journey on!

Insight #906

Periodically give yourself a kick-back day; a day to re-energize, refocus, sharpen your skills, knowledge, and tools. Review your goals, vision, and purpose. Then get back on board your incredible Life's Journey.
Journey on!

Insight #907

Sometimes in life, other, often good-intentioned people may hurt you. That produces frustration and despair even though it was not your fault or action that caused this. Goodness, justice, and moving to a higher level is coming!
Journey on!

Insight #908

Negativity, put-downs, lack of support, and naysayers will only become "show stoppers" if you allow it. The show must go on! Do it! Carry on!
Journey on!

Sharpen

Insight #909

Your inner journey will last your entire life. It will define, direct, and determine your destiny if you just let it out.
Journey on!

Insight #910

A failure, a drop, or a fall is not the end of your journey. Those moments should not be filled with discouragement but anticipation of where you will be going. Stay the course!
Journey on!

Insight #911

Powerful, purposeful individuals always seem to find time for "self." That balance in life is necessary to recharge, redirect, and refocus on what really matters.
Journey on!

Insight #912

You are a miracle in progress. Each day it is your choice to make it really a colossal learning experience that will move you forward.
Journey on!

Course

Insight #913

Focus on performance. That is where your words take shape and form the reality you talk about. Your professional and personal success depends upon the performance you choose!
Journey on!

Insight #914

Your feelings and your emotions are the true doorway to your spirit, inner being, and your soul. Pay close attention, for they will drive and direct you to your destiny.
Journey on!

Insight #915

All of the events and moments you experience on your journey have their own way of falling into a meaningful and purposeful order as you move forward. They will form and reveal your destiny.
Journey on!

Insight #916

There are many big frogs in little ponds. Do not let them deter you from your chosen path. Oh, they will certainly try with their negativity, put downs, criticism, and ongoing chatter. Stay focused and stay your course!
Journey on!

Order

Insight #917

Create an environment that is conducive to supporting you in a positive, supportive, creative manner. That will fire up and release your internal motivation to move forward.
Journey on!

Insight #918

Do not quit, back off, turn away, or give up. Charge forward, be persistent, courageous, jump into the game of life, and be a player. It's your turn, your move—take it!
Journey on!

Insight #919

Each step forward is an ongoing process of discovery. However, you must be the one to take that step in the direction of your future. Do it!
Journey on!

Insight #920

You must learn to be receptive to your inner being. That voice urges you onward. Trust it. You will rise to levels never even imagined!
Journey on!

Conducive

Conducive

Insight #921

There will be moments when you feel overwhelmed. Break what is before you down into smaller parts and take on one at a time. Soon you will feel back in control.

Journey on!

Insight #922

Turn your fears into a driving, productive force to overcome the challenges before you. Soon you will realize that it was just False Evidence Appearing to be Real and you have conquered it.

Journey on!

Insight #923

Do not be so busy that you neglect taking care of yourself. Food, friends, family, learning, loving, and living all must be in balance or you will not be able to carry on.

Journey on!

Insight #924

Take the time each day for personal reflection and the opportunity to listen to that inner spirit. It has important messages and lessons to share. Don't miss them!

Journey on!

Personal

Insight #925

Do not be defined by others. Identifying and understanding your whole self will define the essence of who you are. Then take action. Make it real!

Journey on!

Insight #926

Your destiny is your destiny. It awaits only you. No one else may walk your path, your journey, your future. Claim it!

Journey on!

Insight #927

A magnificent performance awaits and you are the star. The play is "The Story of My Life." You have written the script, selected the supporting actors, and the show must go on! Curtain!

Journey on!

Insight #928

You will make mistakes and some of them will be huge! Welcome to the human race. Now, dare to get back up, move forward, and accomplish your goals!

Journey on!

Define

Insight #929

Your potential is unlimited. What you will achieve and the abundance that awaits you knows no ceiling other than what you set for yourself. Reach, stretch, strive, and bring your future to life.

Journey on!

Insight #930

Feeling too old, too tired, too discouraged? Try this: I am still viable, strong, energized, positive, persistent, and the experience and wisdom I possess is priceless. There is still so much that lies before me and I will move forward.

Journey on!

Insight #931

It is about to happen! Be ready to embrace your destiny. Meaningful results, extraordinary events, and growth you never imagined are taking place. Seize them all!

Journey on!

Insight #932

Awaken to each new day before you and all that will unfold. Get up, get out, and continue on that journey of your life. Behold your destiny!

Journey on!

Seize

Insight #933

What do you have to lose if you stretch beyond your boundaries? You lose only mediocrity, stagnation, and complacency. Focus on what is to be gained: growth, abundance, success, new levels of achievement. Don't stay where you are; move forward to where your future resides.

Journey on!

Insight #934

Keep searching, questioning, examining, challenging, and increasing your knowledge, skills, and ability to continue on! When you believe there is nothing else to be learned, you will be right and begin to wither and self-destruct. You never stop growing, learning, living, and loving until the day you die!

Journey on!

Insight #935

Huge opportunities are out there waiting for your discovery. Stay your course and these items will reveal themselves along your path. Then seize and embrace them!

Journey on!

Insight #936

Every step you take is significant. Nothing is wasted. Even the bad, unfortunate, sad, disappointments serve a purpose in your growth and ultimate good.

Journey on!

Potential

Insight #937

Willpower, trust, faith, permission, fulfillment of purpose, vision, and goals will each promote you when you embrace them and act! Professional and personal wholeness await you!

Journey on!

Insight #938

You have all you need to begin and to continue your journey. It is right there within you. Release it! Let it radiate outward, moving you forward.

Journey on!

Insight #939

The tough times will happen. Part of our reality as human beings is that it will not always go smoothly. Learn and grow and you will be strengthened.

Journey on!

Insight #940

You will overcome the challenges before you if you realize that these obstacles serve a purpose in your journey. They are there to stretch and promote you to an even higher level of success.

Journey on!

Willpower

Willpower

Running harder doesn't help if you're running in the wrong direction!

Insight #941

Keep doing the right things. Do not deviate from your charted course. You will come through the storms that surround you and your future will reveal itself.

Journey on!

Insight #942

Proper planning will prepare you for the performance required to promote you to that next level and beyond.

Journey on!

Insight #943

Use all that you have experienced. Learn from it and build upon it. Make that foundation a benefit to lift you to higher levels.

Journey on!

Insight #944

Do what needs to be done! Give yourself permission to get started right now! That initial forward movement will create a momentum that is unstoppable!

Journey on!

Complacency

Insight #945

Impossible simply means that you haven't found the solution yet. Keep on, persevere, and do not take your focus off of your destiny.

Journey on!

Insight #946

You may be struggling and discouraged. Know that your efforts, focus, determination, and courage will pay off. A turn of events will take place and abundance awaits you!

Journey on!

Insight #947

Do not allow distractions along your journey to take your focus off of things that should matter most. Maintain a sense of urgency.

Journey on!

Insight #948

Did you ever fall over when learning to ride a bike? Did you quit, give it up, never ride again? No! You got back up, got back on, and peddled away to success! Keep on peddling!

Journey on!

Rise Up

Insight #949

It is not a problem when you try and fail, learn, and try again. However, you do yourself a great disservice when you never try at all. Life is not a spectator sport. Get in the game!
Journey on!

Insight #950

Struggles are a part of life. Keep moving onward each day knowing that you are a constant work in progress. Stepping up and moving forward with your life is a key to your destiny.
Journey on!

Insight #951

Are you prepared on the inside—your heart, caring, values, willingness to change and adapt to all you encounter? Keep on moving forward. That is a secret of the universe!
Journey on!

Insight #952

Forgive but do not forget past mistakes and failures. Learn from them so as not to repeat. Don't dwell on that which you cannot change but focus on a purposeful journey to your future.
Journey on!

Sunshine

Insight #953

When you give yourself permission to act, you are all in—committed, involved, focused, determined, with mind, body, and soul.

Journey on!

Insight #954

You are walking along with many others as you progress on your journey. Respect the dignity and the genius of every individual.

Journey on!

Insight #955

Your time has come. Move forward, embrace your future, and make a meaningful difference for yourself and your world!

Journey on!

Insight #956

Are you surrounding yourself with those who will move you forward on your path or leading you in directions that compromise what you know is right? Stay true to yourself, your beliefs, and your focus of attention.

Journey on!

Committed

Insight #957

Meaningful results do not just usually happen. They are the result of your inner convictions radiating outward in your performance and daily actions. It all begins there in your heart.

Journey on!

Insight #958

There are special people in your life you can count on to lift you up and care. Anytime at all, you can call upon them and they will be there.

Journey on!

Insight #959

Hold true to your convictions. When you have items to accomplish that will move you forward, stay that course and do the work required. Do not waiver from the path you have set.

Journey on!

Insight #960

You want to win, grow, learn, and live a purposeful journey. Then step up and into your future. It awaits you and only you can take this incredible trip!

Journey on!

Devoted

Devoted

Take the "right" road to memorable.
Let the average be "left" behind.

RE Hollis

Insight #961

Live a long and prosperous life. Seize every precious moment with your entire being. Embrace with love those who are near and dear to you. Respect the dignity and genius of every single person and never be too comfortable or satisfied. Keep on reaching for more and stretching your boundaries.
Journey on!

Insight #962

Who doesn't want to be leading a life of fulfillment, accomplishment, and having a purposeful journey? Celebrate what you are doing and continue to move forward.
Journey on!

Insight #963

Your dreams are your dreams. Only you can awaken those dreams and bring them to reality. You hold the power of permission. Give it to yourself and accept your destiny.
Journey on!

Insight #964

You may be exhausted as you make your way along your journey. Your hard work, dedication, and focus will give you that additional push to finish strong.
Journey on!

Push

Insight #965

So where are you in your journey right now? Are you moving forward, at a standstill, fallen, or turning back? It is so easy to stop, give up, turn away from your right future. Your strength and determination will allow you to stay the course and take that next step forward.

Journey on!

Insight #966

Excuses, excuses, excuses! You may be good at those. However, there is no reason for them. They keep you from moving forward and stepping up to do what you know you should be doing. Stop holding yourself back with excuses.

Journey on!

Insight #967

This portion of your journey is sponsored by your willingness, knowledge, attitude, health, and joy. Keep on keeping on!

Journey on!

Insight #968

What has been holding you back is about to come to an end. Abundance and success will be yours. All you need to do is to pick up that key of change, new habits, goals, purpose, or vision and put the key into the door to your future and turn it. Open the door and step through. A new level of your destiny awaits you.

Journey on!

Key

Insight #969

Think, do, act, invent, dream, build, open doors, and enjoy every moment of your life-long learning experience. This is your time, your moment to shine. Seize it!

Journey on!

Insight #970

Life is about so much more than making money. God, family, friends, relationships, love, kindness, respect, and the way you live your life all make your way wherever your journey takes you.

Journey on!

Insight #971

Life can come to an immediate halt at any moment in time. Fly high and embrace every second of your precious time. Your journey is a gift and every step you take forward unwraps this gift and shares it with your world. Be and give as much as you can for as long as you can. Eternal rest will give you plenty of time to catch up on your sleep. Right now awaken and live!

Journey on!

Insight #972

You want to be heard—speak! You intend to have things happen—take action! You want to care—display it! You want to demonstrate your love—embrace life! If you allow yourself to have the will to do it, it will happen.

Journey on!

Courage

Insight #973

You have so many special guests you will encounter along your journey—family, friends, coaches, teachers, mentors, clergy, guides, counselors, and significant others, all with their own personal genius and gifts. Embrace and love them!
Journey on!

Insight #974

Are you "locked in" for life when it comes to your purpose, core values, and vision? If so, you have a clear path to your future. Decisions you are faced with are easier to make when in alignment with the directional beacon guiding you and keeping you on course.
Journey on!

Insight #975

Things can change in a heartbeat. Will what you are doing right now will help you to be prepared to meet any challenge, overcome any obstacle, and continue upon your chosen path?
Journey on!

Insight #976

When this you see—think of me. You have left a lasting imprint in the sands of your Life's Journey. Those who follow will feel your presence and all you have accomplished. Rejoice!
Journey on!

Alignment

Insight #977

The difficult choice is to not get involved with life, to hold back, not step forward, to be a spectator, and avoid taking any risks. What a life of mediocrity, uncertainty, and virtual obscurity awaits you. Get involved, be amazing, start now!

Journey on!

Insight #978

Surround yourself with spectacular friends, beautiful moments, an abundance of laughter, and tears of joy! Embrace those you know, like, trust, admire, and respect. You will constantly be lifted up to higher levels of personal and professional success!

Journey on!

Insight #979

Stop being shackled to your past. Realize that you have been holding the key that will release you to move on to your right future.

Journey on!

Insight #980

The sky is the same wherever you go. You should be able to find your happiness where you stand and build the right future.

Journey on!

Mediocrity

Mediocrity

Noah didn't wait for his ship to come in, he built one!

RE Hollis

Insight #981

That place where you feel safe, secure, at peace, and is a comfort to you—an inner sanctum, deep within your very being, is where the spark of purposeful growth ignites.
Journey on!

Insight #982

The one thing in life that is inevitable, that you know you can count on, that *will* happen, is change itself. However, when you prepare your inner core to have a purposeful journey, the changes become secondary to your primary reality.
Journey on!

Insight #983

Your inner being, spirit, and enthusiasm is incredibly important to your very existence. It completes you, providing strength and balance.
Journey on!

Insight #984

Are you willing to admit your minuses as well as embrace your strengths? When you look at the "real you," that awareness becomes an effective force to grow and nurture.
Journey on!

Sanctum

Insight #985

What are those things that you will accomplish this day that will lift you to new heights and places you never even imagined? You need to identify and embrace those items in your life.

Journey on!

Insight #986

When you grasp and understand your purpose, you have power! You now know where you are going and nothing will prevent you from that rendezvous with destiny.

Journey on!

Insight #987

Remove the facade. You must confront the real you before you can move forward with honor. When you face your own reality, you then have shed all the shackles of untruth. It takes humility, honesty, and a willingness to acknowledge the real you.

Journey on!

Insight #988

Seek out role models. Continuously have an insatiable hunger for knowledge and the genius that each person has to share.

Journey on!

Honesty

Insight #989

First, accept responsibility and then you will begin to rebuild your life. You cannot build on a shaky foundation. It must be strong and solid as you construct your future.

Journey on!

Insight #990

Take the time to truly experience what you are living. Look back, but move forward as you discover the real you.

Journey on!

Insight #991

If you are strong enough, determined enough, courageous, and purposeful in your actions, you will transition your dreams into a beautiful reality, your destiny, your right future.

Journey on!

Insight #992

Don't let a bump in the road divert you from your chosen path. Keep your sights on your directional beacon. Your purpose, vision, and goals will lead you.

Journey on!

Construct

Insight #993

Shame, sorrow, and guilt can all be dealt with when you are able to admit your faults and be real. Stop pretending.
Journey on!

Insight #994

There are times when you will not realize the "real" you until you actually are in that moment experiencing and living it. Only then do you discover where the real lies and embrace the truth.
Journey on!

Insight #995

Get honest with yourself. Quit making excuses and face the real you. Realize and accept your humanity. Now, be amazing!
Journey on!

Insight #996

Here is a challenge: hold on to your positive attitude even during the difficult storms you encounter. Each moment becomes a learning experience to complement your life.
Journey on!

Admit

Insight #997

Are you willing to admit your limitations and weaknesses as well as embrace your strengths? When you look at the "real you," that awareness becomes an effective force to grow and nurture.

Journey on!

Insight #998

There will be discouragement, mistakes, disappointments, and setbacks that strike like a hurricane. Don't ever relinquish your dream. You will come through the storm.

Journey on!

Insight #999

Share the story that only you can tell. We learn from one another's experiences and will grow from them if we give ourselves permission to act!

Journey on!

Insight #1,000

There are 1,000 ways in 1,000 days to enlighten, energize, and nurture your inner spirit. You then must allow that force to radiate outward in the daily actions taken in achieving your right future.

Journey on!

Act

Act

Life is a great big canvas and you should throw all the paint you can on it.

R E Hollis

Awareness Promotes Effectiveness

Abundance come to me!

Abundance come to me. I expect it, desire it, and feel the good vibrations of its approach.

Abundance come to me. I sense its presence. It is all around me waiting to be embraced.

Abundance come to me. The joy abounds and I will celebrate my victory.

Abundance come to me.

Abundance come to me. I expect it, desire it, and feel the good vibrations of its approach. I sense its presence. It is all around me waiting to be embraced.

Abundance come to me. The joy abounds and I will celebrate my victory.

Special occasions will take place. You are to discover new things about yourself that will call you to something greater, a higher level where you will encounter experiences to strengthen the direction you have set even more firmly than it was. Strive to achieve your purpose, that universal calling of the path you will follow on your Life's Journey. You will encounter a calling in your life. Whatever path you choose will position you for your destiny. What an incredible decision you have to make. It is your calling, your choice, your life.

About the Authors

Rose D. Sloat and **Darryl S. Doane—The #1 Guides to Professional and Personal Wholeness** are managing partners of The Learning Service, Ltd. They are bestselling authors and international performance-based training and development specialists. They focus on numerous critical issues which include: exceptional customer service, sales effectiveness, leadership and managerial skills development, interpersonal relationships, executive coaching, and long-term performance improvement. They offer a wide variety of educational formats. "Our programs impact performance by supplying the necessary tools for individuals to change their own behavior." "We provide value and produce results."

Rose and Darryl are co-authors of eleven books through HRD Press and AMACOM (The American Management Association).

They are the former Publishers and Primary Content providers for an online magazine: *Life's Journey—Professional & Personal Wholeness*™.

Contact information:

    The Learning Service, Ltd.: Phone: 330-456-2422
    E-mail: learningservice@sbcglobal.net
    Website: www.thelearningservice.com
    Facebook: www.facebook.com/thelearningservice
    Twitter: www.twitter.com/thelearningserv

About the Illustrator

Roger Hollis, President of Roger E. Hollis LLC, is a consultant providing sales management, stra-tegic planning, and business growth planning. Roger has an Associate Degree in Machine Design and a Bachelor of Science Degree in Education. His career included 30+ years in the corporate world with Engineering, Operations and Sales Management experience. He is also a USAF veteran with two tours of duty and 150 combat missions. His avocations include running, the occasional 5K race, volunteering for the Akron Marathon, gardening, and a monthly cartoon illustration for the digital magazine "Life's Journey."

When not working or doodling with this cartoon hobby, as a health advocate, you'll likely see him out running the roads or the trails five to six times a week.

Roger can be reached at:

Roger E. Hollis, 5669 Deer Pines Drive, Clinton, OH 44216
Cellphone: 330-224-2961
E-mail: rehollis8@gmail.com
Offering Value, Quality, and Service to support your needs
See my LinkedIn profile at: http://www.linkedin.com/in/rogerhollisllc

www.ingramcontent.com/pod-product-compliance
Lightning Source LLC
Chambersburg PA
CBHW082108230426
43671CB00015B/2631